SEWING

EVEN A MONKEY CAN DO

A QUICK AND EASY GUIDE TO HELP YOU LEARN HOW TO SEW IN 1 DAY

(INCLUDES 10 PROJECTS WITH STEP BY STEP INSTRUCTIONS AND IMAGES)

Written by Jacob Jensen

JACOB JENSEN

© Copyright Jacob Jensen 2020 - All rights reserved.

The content contained within this book may not be reproduced, duplicated or transmitted without direct written permission from the author or the publisher.

Under no circumstances will any blame or legal responsibility be held against the publisher, or author, for any damages, reparation, or monetary loss due to the information contained within this book. Either directly or indirectly. You are responsible for your own choices, actions, and results.

Legal Notice:
This book is copyright protected. This book is only for personal use. You cannot amend, distribute, sell, use, quote or paraphrase any part, or the content within this book, without the consent of the author or publisher.

Disclaimer Notice:
Please note the information contained within this document is for educational and entertainment purposes only. All effort has been executed to present accurate, up to date, and reliable, complete information. No warranties of any kind are declared or implied. Readers acknowledge that the author is not engaging in the rendering of legal, financial, medical or professional advice. The content within this book has been derived from various sources. Please consult a licensed professional before attempting any techniques outlined in this book.

By reading this document, the reader agrees that under no circumstances is the author responsible for any losses, direct or indirect, which are incurred as a result of the use of the information contained within this document, including, but not limited to, — errors, omissions, or inaccuracies.

SEWING EVEN A MONKEY CAN DO

Sewing even a monkey can do :)

Table of Contents

Introduction 9
Chapter 1: What Is Sewing? 14
   What Is Sewing? 14
   Reasons to Take Up Sewing 15
   What Are Your Sewing Goals? 19
Chapter 2:
Basics of Sewing Machines 20
   Types of Sewing Machines 20
   Grouping Sewing Machines by Functionality 22
   Parts of the Sewing Machine 24
   How to Choose a Sewing Machine 26
   What to Know Before Buying an Old Sewing Machine 28
Chapter 3:
Types of Sewing 30
   Machine Sewing 30
   Hand Sewing 31
   Embroidery 32
   Cross-Stitching 33
   Appliqué 34
Chapter 4:
Tools You Need to Get Started 36
   What to Include in Your Hand Sewing Kit 36
   How to Create Your Own Machine Sewing Kit 43
   Storage 46
   How to Choose the Right Fabric 48

Cutting Tools 51
Pressing Tools 52

Chapter 5:
Basic Sewing Patterns 56
Basting 56
Back Stitching 58
Whip Stitch 61
Basic Cross-Stitch 63

Chapter 6:
Getting Ready to Sew 66
You Are Ready to Sew! 66
Threading Your Machine 67
How to Prepare the Fabric 71
Prepare the Pattern 73
How to Cut the Fabric 74
Selecting a Pattern 75
Pattern layout 76
Cutting Line 77
Marking 77
Sewing a Seam 78
Threading and Tension 79
Threading the Bobbin 80
Tension 81
Start Stitching 82
How to Use the Hand Wheel 83

Chapter 7:
Taking Accurate Measurements 87
Preparations before Sewing 87
Pillow Cover Measurements 91
Garment Measurements 92
How to Take Accurate Body Measurements 96

Chapter 8:
Common Mistakes Sewing Beginners Make 98
   Starting on a really expensive sewing machine 98
   Using the wrong tools on a project 99
   Working on more than one project at a go 99
   Buying patterns that have to be altered 100
   Buying a lot of things before getting started 100
   Downloading complex patterns with no guide 101
   Not taking time to learn a sewing machine 101
   Ignoring fabric suggestions on patterns 102

Chapter 9:
Using Your Machine's Stitch Functions 103

Chapter 10:
The Special Techniques of Sewing 108
   Hemming 108
   Use of two threads to create a gathering 109
   Appliqué work 110
   French seam 112
   Flat-felled seams 112
   Bias bound seams 113
   Using a rotary cutter 113
   Princess seams 114
   Pressing and ironing 114
   Clipping corners and curves 115
   Stay stitching 115
   Fussy cutting 116
   Use of bar tracks 116

Chapter 11:
Machine Maintenance 117
   Procedure of Sewing Machine Maintenance 117
   Accessories Required for Maintenance 119

Chapter 12:
Troubleshooting Common Sewing Problems 121
    Can you repair your sewing machine if it encounters minor problems? 121
    Grandma's Sewing Hacks 122

Chapter 13:
10 Sewing Projects **124**
    Oven Gloves 124
    Tablecloth 133
    Fabric Storage Box 142
    Multi-Purpose Tool Organizer 148
    Plain Shirt 157
    Basic Pajama Pants 160
    Hot Water Bottle Cover 164
    Table Runner 172
    Red Carpet Dress in 20 Minutes 178
    Multi-Purpose Bag 180

Conclusion **193**

Introduction

Life had suddenly and very unexpectedly come crashing down around me. However, I'm getting ahead of myself. There I was, married, two years in, having just been promoted eight months prior and moving into my third career position on the East Coast. These were exciting times; 7 figures of responsibility, 27 clients to consult with, and we'd purchased our first house! Wow, life was a whirlwind of things getting better and better and better. My bride and I had just settled into our neighborhood, she'd landed a job, we'd found a house of worship to attend, life was good.

However, after two-plus weeks in a battle with what I thought was the flu, my life came crashing down. It was one of those drag you down, beat you up, not going to let you up out of bed types of illness. Everything ached! I had never slept 20 hours a day before. I knew I needed to get myself to the doctor's office immediately. There, they did blood tests, gave me a basic physical, and sent me to the hospital for another set of tests.

At the hospital, I was X-rayed and asked to stay around. A small team of medical professionals arrived within 30 minutes, and I was hustled into the ultrasound waiting room and bumped to the front of the line, ahead of all those pregnant ladies. There, they all crammed themselves into the room, and as the ultrasound was done once, twice, three times, I finally received a diagnosis. I was asked to drive directly to my gastroenterologist's office and was told he was waiting for me. Plus, oh yes, "We have an appointment for you with your family doctor tomorrow at 9:00 a.m. Please be there; don't miss it."

Just over an hour later, my gastroenterologist informed me I had cancer in my lower digestive tract. Ouch. The next morning my family doctor told me she had been working the phones.

I'd just left the surgeon's office after being told I had cancer, in shock, yet all my life I was raised to assess, research, and reassess, then create a plan of action, then take action. I got back to my car. There, I had a big cry of crocodile sized tears. Then, I knew it was time to take action. I drove to the family lawyer's office, where I got a new will drawn up. My last one was two years old and done in another province. I recognized it was essential to have the proper paperwork up to date, to be safe, and to make things easier for my spouse.

Now the tea was cool enough to drink. *A plan. A plan. What do I need? What do we need? Support?* I was already blessed to have a loving spouse, parents, siblings, and wonderful coworkers. What was next? Isolation in the hospital for several weeks. So, as I'd been taught, build a team. Ask for help. Ask for what you need.

Well, that caused a dam to burst. It was very remarkable as the notes, cards, letters, and plants all started to arrive at my home. Talk about sharing hope!

A key thing that helped me fight my cancer was building a team, asking for help, and specifying what I wanted during my battles and challenges ahead. Their gifts of notes, cards, pictures, flowers, and so much more brought encouragement. To this day, it takes my breath away. Each person offered me hope, each helped me focus on the now, and each person helped me recognize that I'm resilient! Very powerful. This is how I turned Hopelessness into Hopefulness. You can also do the same by reading this book.

Do you know that you can stitch a pillowcase (even napkin pillowcases) in 30 minutes by hand and 15 minutes on a sewing machine?

Want to know what sewing actually is and how you can become a master in it? This book is a tutorial for all the newbies in the field of sewing. In this book, you will learn the quickest and easiest methods of sewing.

Sewing is an exemplary artistic skill for your hands. Your sewing passion could have popped up by using a tutorial guide. If you're a raw newbie, then you will never learn the sewing of your dreams without a direct guide and true tutorial. This book teaches you the right and easiest way of sewing dresses and stuff like pajamas and pants.

This book is well researched and teaches you various tips to making sewing handy for you. You can learn about hand sewing tips, hand sewing techniques, and hand sewing stitches.

I have put forth everything you need to choose the best and most comfortable sewing tools that befit your nature. From simple burp cloths to expert trendy skirts, with this book you can be the be-all and end-all of sewing.

You can learn from simple to complex and from specific to general tactics of sewing. You will come away with novel ideas and be astounded with the many methods of stitching.

This book is best for those who want to become a sewing master. Here you will learn how to make your sewing kit perfect and most functional. Moreover, in this book you will gain knowledge about the various patterns of sewing, their importance, and the things needed to make patterns. You can learn how you can make your sewing easier with the help of sewing patterns. Patterns give you a direction and allow you to copy the design whenever you want.

The thing is that sewing is an important life skill you need to know so that you can make the necessary repairs on your clothing and make simple projects to add customized flare to your house. It is considered such an important skill that children all over the world were once taught how to sew at a young age by their parents or as part of their lessons in school. If you want to learn how to sew, then this book will definitely serve as your guide on how to start sewing.

Sewing is an important life skill. With sewing, you will be able to make your own clothes and home décor. You will also be able to fix damaged clothes and extend the life of your clothes. Learning how to sew is very easy, and you can start with just a few materials like needles, threads and fabric. By learning the basics of sewing, you will be able to make a lot of things out of a piece of fabric.

Sewing is one of those handicrafts that can take on numerous forms and variations. Sewing can be a livelihood, a craft, a hobby, a way that you make repairs. It can be a necessity, and it can also be something you do simply for enjoyment. It can also be an art form, and a way that you express yourself through the mediums of fabric and thread. For many people, sewing can also be considered a life skill because you can use it to enhance your life in so many ways, whether through decorating your home or clothing your body. Sewing can be fun, rewarding, and easy once you get going.

At the end of this book, you'll find instructions for simple sewing projects from crafts to clothing so that you can try out your new skills for yourself. Once you've given them a try, you'll be in a good place to begin branching out into a variety of other sewing types and projects all your own. You'll also have a sense of how to sew without using a paper pattern, so you can feel free to begin designing things that you dream up, rather than just settling for things that someone else has already created.

So, kick back, pick up this book, and become a sewing master. Follow along in the book to understand the basic patterns and stitching styles. You will dig up new methods and explore the easiest sewing tips from this book.

Happy sewing!

Chapter 1:

What Is Sewing?

What Is Sewing?

Sewing is the art of stitching a fabric with needle and thread, which was first discovered by humans in the Paleolithic age. History also dates this as the same time when prehistoric technological roots in human evolution took shape. For some people, the knack of sewing is innate because they have watched their mothers or friends sewing. It can seem a tad daunting at first; nevertheless, the truth is, with the zillions of sewing types, styles and options, you will find one that befits your interests easily!

Often, it is good for a beginner to start with hand stitching, as it prepares the mind for the practical process of how sewing actually happens. While hand stitching itself has its own versions of continuous stitching and embroidery, there are superb sewing machines and accessories to lessen the drudgery you experience while sewing for hours manually with your hands!

Regardless of whether you are an idiot at sewing or a returning sewing learner, this is an art with overwhelming creativity. It brings forth the patience, beauty and knack for intricacy in every person. Sewing is not just for the tailors because from sewing pillowcases to exquisite bedspreads, there are zillions of sewing options to fit whatever your comfort zone is. Sewing is one of the top voted hobbies fit for all ages, as it is therapeutic too.

Sewing is a skill that traditionally only women and homemakers learned. Today, so much has changed, and everyone wants to learn as many essential skills as possible if it means that they can improve their lives. Sewing is a great skill to master for its many benefits, not just so that you can easily mend your clothes but also in order to enjoy the fun involved in exploring creativity and making new garments.

Reasons to Take Up Sewing

There are a lot of reasons why you may want to consider taking up sewing; however, regardless of what you want to do with your finished results and beyond having the skills necessary to complete any kind of project that catches your eye, you can also:

- Improve your hand-eye coordination
- Learn to blend color and make art or decorations with a very different medium
- Copy expensive or designer clothes or costumes for less money
- Start a small side business making crafts, bags, clothes, or accessories

- Express yourself through fabric
- Have something to do with your hands during downtime
- Learn a relaxing skill that keeps your hands busy while your mind is free

Best of all, you'll be learning a new skill that can challenge you and give you a great sense of accomplishment. After all, there's nothing quite like finishing a project like a new skirt and trying it on for the first time, or completing a new set of curtains or a new slipcover that can transform a room of your home in just minutes.

Sewing is also a skill that will help you save money, as purchasing clothing can be quite expensive. You can also count on the therapeutic nature of sewing, as you begin a task with odds and ends which do not go well together and end the task with a garment that looks brilliant. Here are some other reasons why you might want to explore sewing.

TO EXPLORE YOUR INDEPENDENCE

When you can create your own clothing, you are able to enjoy a certain level of independence. In case you need to attend a function or you require a special outfit on short notice, you are not restricted to trying to find a shop that is open or somewhere to make a purchase. You can simply create what you want to wear, ensuring that you maintain a unique look at a moment's notice.

SEWING HELPS PROTECT THE ENVIRONMENT
Being able to sew provides you with the perfect opportunity to repurpose materials and create unique items for a range of purposes. This saves you from having to purchase new materials or throw away the ones you have which may be suited for another item. Things like curtains can easily be converted into cushion covers, and even an old pair of jeans can make an excellent pair of shirts with a matching bag. All this is possible if you know how to sew.

SEWING IS COST EFFECTIVE
Sewing will not only save you money when it comes to making clothing, but there are so many other items that you can sew as well. You can create special items to use for the décor of your home, including curtains and tablecloths, or create a range of crafts. With skill in sewing, you do not have to worry about purchasing gifts for others; you can create personalized gifts with ease.

SEWING ALLOWS YOU TO CREATE YOUR OWN PERSONAL STYLE
Many people like to have a unique look, a style which stands out and helps them be identified as individuals. Having the ability to sew makes it possible to define the way you want to look so that you never need to worry that you will resemble another person when you step out of your home. If you do have clothes that you bought earlier, you will find you can easily

amend them to make them more suited to you if you have adequate knowledge of sewing.

SEWING ALLOWS YOU TO REPLICATE

Have you ever seen a stunning design for a garment on a runway and known that you cannot afford to purchase it? If you know how to sew, you can look at it and draw inspiration to create your own garment that is similar. Furthermore, many clothes are made in sizes that are generic for models but may not be ideal for the actual person who is meant to wear the item. When you know how to sew, you can ensure that you create a clothing item that will fit you well all over your body so that you can make the best of your physique.

GO AGAINST THE STEREOTYPES

Things have changed, and now more men are taking up sewing, as can be seen by the numerous clothes designers that have shared their collections. Nowadays, sewing is a means of exploring your creativity, and the gender bias is quickly dissipating.

SEWING SKILLS WILL ALWAYS BE RELEVANT

No matter where you may be in the world, and whatever your social standing is, knowing how to sew will always be an advantage. This is because people everywhere need to have clothes to cover their bodies and can also use these skills to earn revenue.

SEWING FEELS GREAT

When you have completed a sewing project that you were working on, you will have a sense of accomplishment and will feel great for getting the job done. What would be even better is if you wear your item in public and receive some praise for it. As sewing is a skill, you will only get better with more practice and the passing of time, and before you know it, you will be able to confidently create any item you require as long as you have access to a needle and thread.

What Are Your Sewing Goals?

Before you begin, make sure you do the things listed below:
- Maintain a personal sewing book
- Set realistic goals for your first project
- Do exactly as the book says for the days mentioned
- Whenever you like a pattern or technique of sewing, make sure to add it to your Sewing Diary or book
- Whenever you add a sewing pattern to your book, pick up a needle and thread and sew a thumbnail image of the same on your page
- Chart your own convenient Metric Table in your sewing area

These are just too many things to take in on the first day, so go ahead and look up everything you have noted down in your Sewing Diary.

Chapter 2:

Basics of Sewing Machines

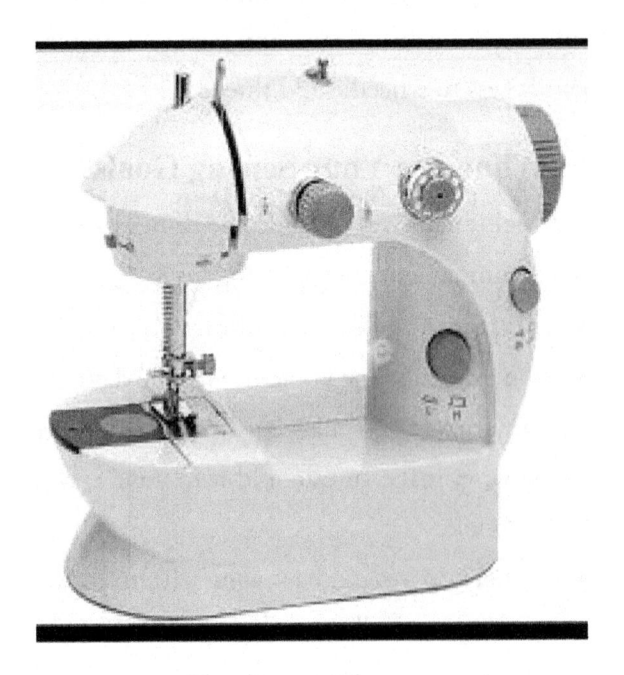

Types of Sewing Machines

If you're going to use a sewing machine for your projects, it's best to make sure you have the best one. These sewing machines will do the trick.

BLUE TIP/SINGER/Q NEEDLE

This machine makes use of a Stretch Needle Point type and is best used to prevent snagging and skipped stitches. This also works best for microfibers and knits, amongst other fabrics.

EUROPEAN 130/705HJ

This machine makes use of the Tightly Woven Fabric system and works best for upholstery, denim, and the heaviest types of corduroys.

AMERICAN 15 X 1DE

These have sharp needles and are best used for sewing jeans, denim, and other heavy fabrics.

130/705H OR 15 X 1DE AMERICAN

This is ideal for a beginner, as it is a universal sewing machine and works for most types of threads and fabrics.

Grouping Sewing Machines by Functionality

STRAIGHT NOSE SEWING MACHINE
They can sew with one, two or three needles. They make closed seams.

OVERLOCK MACHINE
It is also known as Overlock. You can make an overcast stitch, preventing the selvedges from fraying.

COATING MACHINE
The seam of this machine is flat and is ideal for knitting. You can do topstitching and also closed seams.

COLLARED MACHINE
Tape is inserted through a funnel, which is folded for parts of fabric with curved areas such as the neck of a shirt.

BASTERA MACHINE

It makes invisible stitches that are used for hems or hems in skirts and pants.

DOCKING MACHINE

It is used in places where the fabric is subjected to a lot of stretching. Secure pockets.

BUTTON MACHINE

Pastes flat buttons in all ways.

BUTTONHOLE MACHINE

Makes buttonholes and can cut them automatically.

CLOSING MACHINE

It makes a chain stitch with a French stitch and is used to close pants, sleeves, and shirts, among other things.

ELASTIC MACHINE

Applies elastics.

CUTTING MACHINE

Cuts according to a pattern and the depth of a blade.

Parts of the Sewing Machine

GRADUATION WHEEL

This corresponds to the wheel located on the side of the machine. This wheel is rotated and allows you to puncture or remove the needle from the fabric. It is usually very useful when the needle is stuck and must be removed manually.

Sometimes you can use the roulette to start working the machine, instead of using the pedal. This process is considered much slower, but it is certainly safer.

STITCH SELECTION BUTTONS

These buttons allow you to adjust the width and length of the stitch. For this you must select the number according to your needs. If you want to reinforce the stitch you can use zero (0);

with this number you will make several stitches in one place. However, if you want to make short stitches, use number 1 (for example, for a buttonhole). Number 2 is considered normal, and numbers greater than 2 are used for basting stitching.

REVERSE LEVER

Also known as a reverse button. This is used to finish off the seams. For some seams it is customary to reinforce the stitches with reverse seams.

This guarantees the resistance and total finish of the manufactured pieces. It is a very practical utility, especially when getting started in sewing, and when you want to ensure the quality of the garments.

COIL HOLDER

This is where the thread is located, and it is also known as thread tension. According to the thickness of the thread, the small thread must be adjusted, ranging from 0 to 9. Number 4 is considered normal; however, if we are dealing with a thicker or thinner thread, it requires an adjustment.

PRESSER FOOT

After you place the thread into the machine, you will find the presser foot. This can be used through a small lever generally located at the rear of the machine. If you want to thread the needle, you must raise it; to start sewing, you must lower it.

SEWING PLATE
Basically, this is the base where the presser foot and needle are located. The drive teeth are also located in this area.

BOBBIN HOLDERS
This is a small metal drawer that is easily removable. Inside is the bobbin and thread.

How to Choose a Sewing Machine

Let's start at the beginning: how do you know that you are choosing the right sewing machine? Next I am going to give you some tricks to know which sewing machine to buy:

WHAT SEWING LEVEL AM I AT?
If it is the first sewing machine that you have ever bought, the best thing is to buy a machine that is neither too expensive nor too complex because when you start, you do not know if you are going to like it or simply do not know if it will work well for you. Also, just because it is a cheap machine, it does not mean it is bad. If you are already in that phase in which you are sewing with machines from the year your mother was born, and despite the difficulties of it being an old machine, you are good at sewing with it, I recommend you buy a good quality machine, but not an excessively expensive one. If you are already at a very advanced level, surely you have already tried several brands, and you know more or less the brand that best suits you and the benefits you want the machine to have for the jobs you normally do.

WHAT PURPOSE WILL MY SEWING MACHINE HAVE?

That is to say, do you want a machine to sew your own clothes, to sew your neighbors' clothes and do some work, or do you really want to dedicate yourself professionally to sewing? Choosing a machine with more or less motor power depends on the objective that the sewing machine will fulfill. You can check the characteristics of the machine and even look at the technical sheet on the manufacturer's page directly. If you are already a professional and the objective is industrial sewing, then do not worry about it; there are many workshop machines that are great second-hand and at a good price.

WHAT BRAND SHOULD I CHOOSE?

I always say the same thing, but for me these are the best and give quality assurance: Alfa and Singer are my favorites. Brother is not bad either, or if you want a good but somewhat more expensive machine, JUKI is the best.

MECHANICAL OR ELECTRICAL?

Well, here it will depend on taste and how well you know technology. The mechanical machines are simple – no screens, no stories, just wheels, but perhaps the benefits of making programmed or embroidered buttonholes are missing. On the other hand, the electric ones are of a higher range, most with a touch screen, and tend to have more features.

WHAT DO I DO IF I AM STUCK BETWEEN TWO SIMILAR MODELS?

I personally would choose the latest model if the brand is the same. If they are two different brands, it is a matter of taste. I am more of a Singer person, but there are people who prefer Alfa. If you are in doubt, I would look at the power of the motor, as this has a great influence on being able to sew fabrics together, as well as denim and elastic, and ensuring that the drag of the fabric is better and does not hit jumps.

What to Know Before Buying an Old Sewing Machine

Here are some recommendations to take into account when choosing your old sewing machine:

- For a sewing machine to be considered old, its manufacturing date must be before 1900. So, check its history and model well as they will help you to clearly certify the age of the machine.
- Carefully observe the materials with which it is built and the condition it is in. Check the level of deterioration or wear of the mechanical parts, paint and the piece of furniture or drawer in which it is kept.
- Examine the accessories and check if it has the original wooden box, manual, keys and documents. These elements increase the price of the machine.

Make sure that your provider can offer you maintenance service with quality spare parts. Also, find accessories that can help you keep your old sewing machine always in good condition.

Chapter 3:

Types of Sewing

One of the reasons that sewing is such a broad hobby to learn is that there are so many different kinds, and many of these types have subcategories that can branch out in seemingly endless ways, such as the many different kinds of cross-stitch, or the multiple types of embroidery stitches that you can learn.

This basic overview of sewing types will help you get an understanding for what they are, as well as for when you may want to use them.

Machine Sewing

Sewing by machine is a lot faster than attempting the same project by hand, which is why so many people want to learn how to use a sewing machine and figure out what it can do. Your basic sewing machine has a lot of functions. It can:

- Sew straight or curved lines with stitches of varying lengths
- Make zigzag stitches of different sizes and length
- Make loose basting-style stitches that can hold things together temporarily so you can put in more decorative stitching later

Depending on your machine, you may also be able to make decorative top stitching and embroidery as well. And while a standard sewing machine doesn't seem as though it has that many functions, you can use those few functions in a variety of ways to get the finished piece you're after.

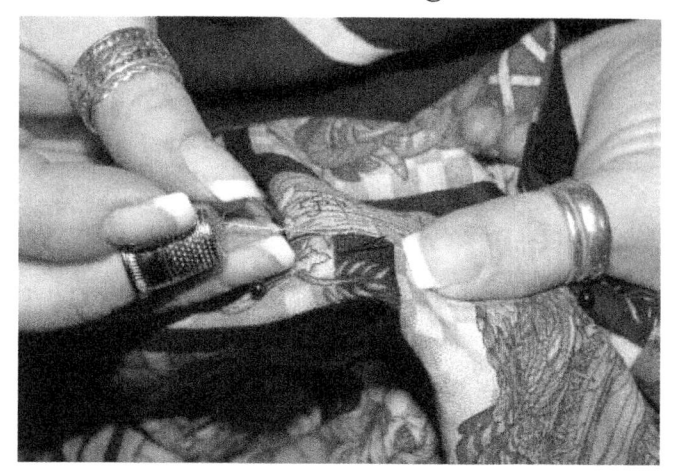

Hand Sewing

Even if you decide that you want to make the majority of your projects by machine, you should still learn a few basic stitches by hand. Why? Some projects may need you to finish a small section by hand, or you may find yourself far from home with a hem that's suddenly fallen and there's no machine to help tack it up. You can also stitch by hand anywhere – from the office, school, the park – bringing along your sewing machine is a lot more awkward and cumbersome than just bringing a needle and some thread.

Embroidery

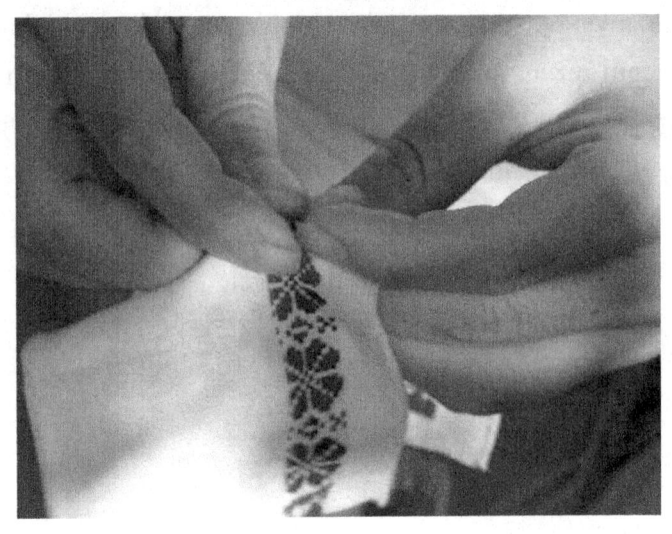

If you want to put your own personal stamp on anything from tablecloths to clothes, embroidery is the way to do it. Embroidery involves making decorative, colorful patterns and images on cloth using a special heavy thread and various types of stitches. Most embroidery involves a variety of different stitches and colors within a pattern. You can use any type of cloth to embroider, and you can also embroider using some specialty sewing machines.

Embroidery can be a fun way to sew your name onto something, stitch the outline of a car onto a toddler's t-shirt, or make a 3D raised design around the collar of a shirt. Once you've learned some basic hand sewing stitches, it's easy to make the jump to embroidery by using some of the same stitches as your starting point and placing them where they can be seen, with a thread and needle large enough to give you the look you're after.

Cross-Stitching

Cross-stitching can also be used to decorate fabric, but it differs from embroidery in a few ways. There are several different cross-stitches, but the basic principle remains the same; you make two stitches per square of fabric, with the two stitches crossing or intersecting with one another in some way.

To achieve this, cross-stitching is usually done on fabric that is easily divided into a grid, such as linen. Cross-stitched patterns can take on many different looks, from abstract colors to detailed scenes, but they all have a similar geometric look based on the grid of the fabric and the nature of the stitches.

Cross-stitching is fairly simple once you get the hang of it, and it can be a relaxing way to add some color and detail to your life. The repetitive nature of the stitches means that you don't have to pay close attention to what you are doing, much like knitting, which makes cross-stitching a great activity for when you're watching TV or waiting for an appointment.

Appliqué

Appliqué is the process of layering pieces of fabric into a pattern. This could be cutting out shapes and attaching them to a shirt, or it could be attaching a decorative border to a set of curtains.

There are a number of ways you can appliqué. The most common involves simply stitching around the edge of a shape to attach it to the one below. Depending on what type of fabric you're using, however, this may not be enough, because the fabric edge could either curl or unravel. To fix this, you can either fold the edge of the decorative piece under before stitching it down, or use a different type of stitch to help cover the edge of the decorative piece to hold it flat and prevent any unraveling.

SEWING EVEN A MONKEY CAN DO

Any type of fabric can be used in appliqué – felt, jersey knit, cotton – you can get very creative with the appliqué process, joining together multiple shapes and colors. I once appliquéd a felt bus onto my son's shirt using embroidery thread and a blanket stitch.

Using appliqué can let you decorate and personalize nearly anything. And because you can use simple stitches or even a sewing machine to do so, anyone can learn to appliqué, no matter what your level of expertise with a needle and thread.

Chapter 4:

Tools You Need to Get Started

So, you want to learn how to sew so that you can start making your own clothes? Before you even pick up a needle and thread, make sure you have everything you need to get started.

What to Include in Your Hand Sewing Kit

Sewing is just like cooking. You need to have all the materials needed in order to create the item that you want to make. There is so much more to sewing than just getting a needle and a spool of thread; thus, it is important that you make a little excursion to the haberdashery shop. But if you are new to sewing, looking at all the choices in front of you can be a little intimidating.

If you are a beginner at sewing, you don't need to get all the tools you see to create beautiful projects. Whether you will be sewing mostly by hand or using a sewing machine, below are the materials that you need to have in your sewing kit.

SEWING NEEDLES

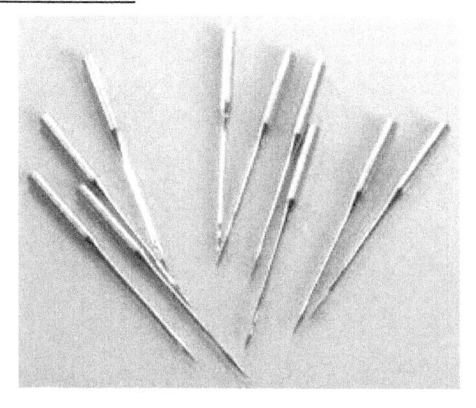

There are different types of needles that are sold for different purposes. Buy a needle set that comes with different types as well as sizes of needles. That way, you will have the right needle for the type of fabric that you want to work with.

PINS

Also called dressmaker pins and all-purpose pins, straight pins are made from stainless steel and are used in pinning different types of fabrics. They may come with round or flat heads. If you are a beginner, round-headed pins are easier to handle.

NEEDLE THREADER

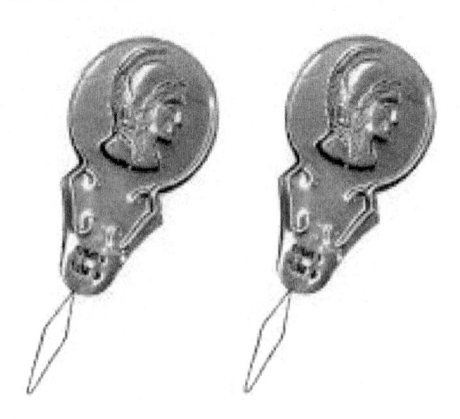

Threading the small eye of a needle can be a daunting task even for expert hobbyists. To save time, it is better to get a needle threader to help you thread your needles easily. This is a metal gadget that comes with a wire loop that goes through the eye of the needle. Insert the thread into the loop and pull it back out. Once you pull it back, the thread will go inside the eye.

SEAM RIPPER

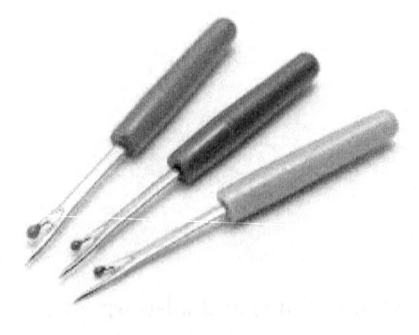

A seam ripper is a tool that allows you to loosen an offending seam so that you can redo your stitches without damaging the fabric.

TAPE MEASURE

Sewing requires you to make the necessary measurements; thus, it is important that you include a measuring tool in your kit. Tape measures often have a total length of 60 inches. Make sure you choose one that comes with imperial measurements on one side and the metric equivalent on the other.

SHEARS

Shears are the best cutting tools for sewing. They are different from scissors in that they have asymmetrical handle sizes, thus providing more leverage when you use it to cut fabric. The handles are also bent upwards, and thus the fabric lies flat on the table during cutting. Never use shears to cut paper because it dulls them.

GRIDDED RULER

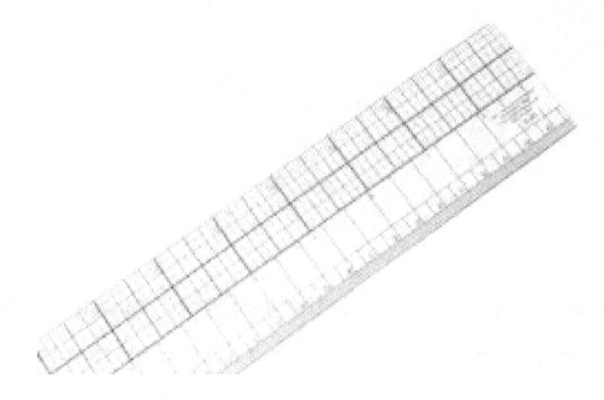

A clear plastic rule is an important material for your sewing kit as it allows you to make a straight line on the fabric.

SHARPENER

Of course, you need a sharpener to make sure that your pencils stay in tip-top shape – literally and figuratively. A regular pencil sharpener will do.

SEAM GAUGE

A seam gauge is a 6-inch long ruler with a sliding gauge that runs the entire length of the ruler. It allows you to make constant seam allowances so you don't run out of fabric when sewing.

FABRIC MARKERS

It is important that you transfer your patterns to the fabric, and this can be achieved using fabric markers. You can buy fabric markers from your haberdashery shop. Make sure you do not substitute them for a pen or pencil because the ink may not easily wash out of the fabric.

THIMBLE

A thimble is a tiny metal cup that fits on your fingertips. Its main function is to protect the fingertips that push the needle when hand sewing so they don't get pricked or bruised over time. People often use this when working with heavy fabrics.

THREAD

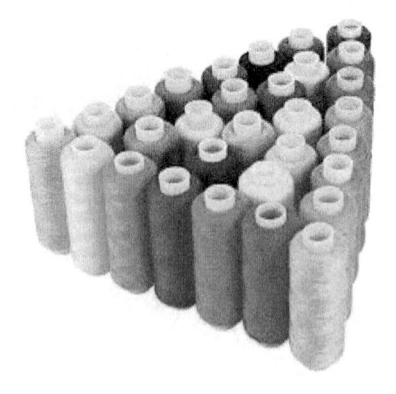

It is important that you get good quality thread for your sewing projects. When choosing the right thread, make sure the color of the thread is similar to the fabric you are working with. Moreover, make sure the thread comes with a smooth finish. Avoid fuzzy threads as they can easily break and may produce lint over time.

How to Create Your Own Machine Sewing Kit

While hand sewing is a great way to create cool projects, there are times when machine sewing is better. This is especially true if you want to make complicated projects within a short span of time. Creating a machine sewing kit is easy. Aside from the basic materials and tools mentioned earlier, below are the other things you need for your machine sewing kit.

SEWING MACHINE

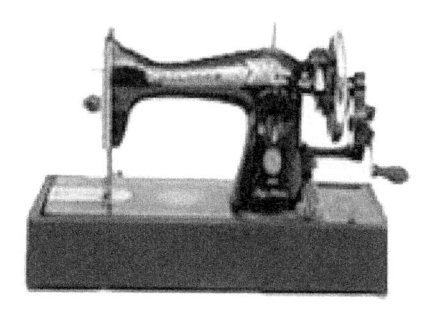

You need a sewing machine, of course. If you are a beginner, choose a sewing machine that has the basic features. You need a decent yet reliable machine that you can use to develop your sewing skills. Do not be persuaded by the salesperson to get an expensive machine that comes with 1,000 stitches. When choosing a sewing machine, think about what you want to do. Do you want to do simple sewing or quilting? Determining your sewing goals can help you decide what kind of sewing machine you need.

BOBBINS

A sewing machine works because the upper and lower threads interlock with each other. While the upper thread sits on the spindle, the lower thread is located in the bobbin. When you buy a sewing machine, it usually provide three bobbins, but it is better if you keep several bobbins handy so that you don't need to unravel a bobbin every time you use a new thread color.

PRESSER FOOT

The presser foot holds the fabric securely while the needle goes in and out of the fabric. The presser foot keeps the fabric stable so that you can evenly stitch on it.

ZIPPER FOOT

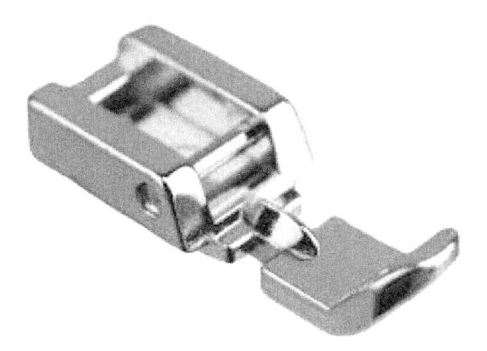

A zipper foot is an important tool that allows you to put a zipper in your sewing project. It is also used in inserting piping as well as cording if you are making home décor like curtains or seat covers.

SCREWDRIVER

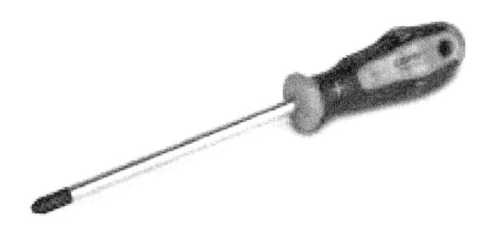

The screwdriver is an important tool when using a sewing machine. You need to use it to loosen or tighten the screw that holds the machine needle in place.

SMALL BRUSH

A small brush allows you to clean the nooks and crannies of your sewing machine. Remember that dust or lint can jam the inner workings of the machine.

Storage

Even though sewing supplies don't occupy much space, it's for this very reason that they can easily get lost. Nothing is more frustrating than not being able to find an item when you need it most. Storage solutions come in many different sizes and budgets. That's why it's not a bad idea to start small first.

A multi-storage box with transparent mini drawers always comes in handy to store the really small stuff. A pincushion keeps your needles where they belong – because the last thing you want is a minefield of needles in your home.

Once the sewing frenzy hits you, the fabrics will start to pile up in your home. At that point you will want to have a clear overview of your fabrics. To do this, you can simply fold your fabrics and place them vertically in boxes. This way you know exactly what fabrics you have and you don't have to make a huge mess while trying to pull out one particular piece.

You can store your fabrics according to whichever category makes most sense to you. It can be by color, type (see "Fabrics") or size.

Silky fabrics don't like to stay neatly folded, but a rubber band can keep them in place.

How to Choose the Right Fabric

Cotton	Velvet	Jersey	Silk	Wool	Denim	Satin
Jacquard	Linen	Rayon	Chiffon	Chenille	Baize	Charmeuse
Cheviot	Dimity	Drill	Felt	Twill	Poplin	Georgette

Using the right fabric is very important in sewing. Buying them can also be addictive. However, before you stock up on fabrics, make sure you know how to choose the right fabric to work with. This section will discuss tips on how to select the right fabric for your sewing projects.

You will realize there are hundreds of fabrics to choose from. If you are a beginner at sewing, it is important that you choose the right fabric that is easy to work with. Below is a list of the different types of fabrics used.

COTTON

Cotton is considered the most versatile fabric and is used to make shirts, skirts, bags and all sorts of sewing projects. It is also fairly cheaper than other fabrics.

COTTON JERSEY

Cotton jersey is knitted by a machine from fine cotton fibers. It has a stretchy characteristic and is also very comfortable to wear. Unfortunately, cotton jersey is not very easy to sew for beginners.

LINEN

Linen is a woven fabric that comes in different weights. It creases a lot, which makes it a bit challenging to work with. It is used to make different types of sundresses and other summer clothes due to its lightweight feel.

SILK

Silk is an expensive woven fabric and it is shiny and has slippery characteristics. It is used to make luxury clothing, and thus it is very expensive. Due to its slipperiness, it can be quite difficult to sew silk.

WOOL

Wool fabric is either knitted or woven. It is made into suits, posh skirts, trousers and coats. It tends to be expensive.

POLYESTER

Synthetic fabrics are lightweight and resistant to creasing. They are also fairly cheap, and thus they are great fabrics for beginners.

Choosing the right fabric can be overwhelming for beginners. To begin with, it is important to choose a fabric that you can practice your sewing skills on, so starting with a relatively cheaper fabric is your best choice. Aside from this factor, below are the other things you need to consider when choosing the right fabric.

Choose woven fabrics because they will not slip or stretch once you sew them. These include cotton or linen. Avoid knitted fabrics because they are difficult to work with.

Select fabrics with plain colors and small prints. Avoid fabrics that have big patterns or stripes because they are very difficult to lay out.

Avoid heavyweight fabrics because they are difficult to manipulate. Heavy fabrics include denim and corduroy.

Deciding which fabric you need to buy is very important. However, shopping for fabrics can become a daunting task. Below are the things you need to do when buying fabrics.

Unroll the fabric just a little to see how it drapes. Try to see how it feels. Does it feel smooth or scratchy? Choose fabrics that have good drape.

Look at the label of the fabric and try to find out the fiber content as well as the care instructions. If you think the fabric is too high maintenance, move to the next one.

Fabrics come in different widths, including 60 inches and 45 inches. Make sure you buy the fabric your pattern needs.

When buying fabrics, it is important that you take your time in choosing the right ones for your sewing projects.

Cutting Tools

Of course, you also need tools for cutting your thread and fabrics for the pieces you will make. Being precise and sharp when it comes to cutting is essential in the line of sewing – and these tools will help you do that and more!

SCISSORS

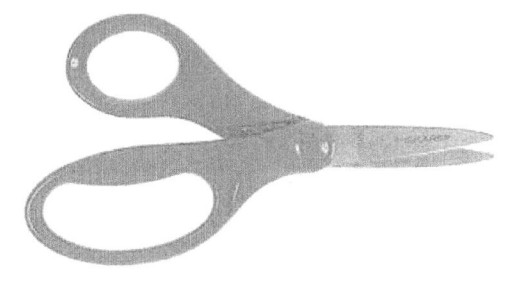

Scissors with bent edges are useful for cutting thread and light fabric, and are handier than shears.

ROTARY CUTTER

Rotary cutters will help you cut fabric and thread in the exact manner that you want, and will help you create straight edges. These are best used for long slices and curves.

SEAM RIPPER

A seam ripper is an inexpensive little tool that comes in handy when you need to reverse your mistakes. As the name suggests, if you see seams in what you're doing, you can undo them with this.

Pressing Tools

Of course, to make your projects cleaner and more presentable, you also need to have some pressing tools.

IRONING BOARD

A regular sized one will do, but keep in mind that it comes in other sizes as well. Aside from being useful for your projects, you know you can use one in your everyday life, too!

STEAM IRON

Choose a reputable brand of iron that heats evenly and has various steam settings to accommodate the range of fabric types you may be using.

MINI IRON

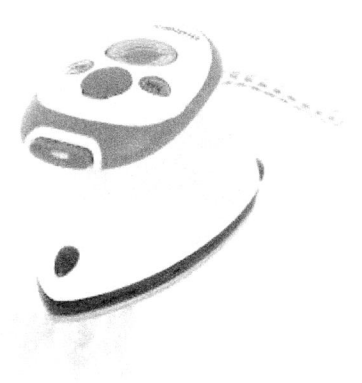

This is meant for smaller, lighter types of fabric that can't handle too much heat.

PRESSING CLOTHS

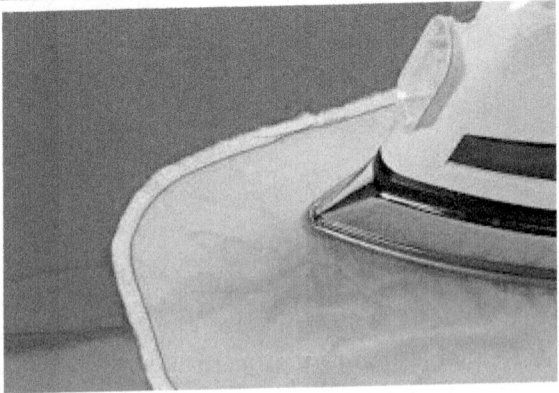

A pressing cloth will prevent unnecessary heating, especially on sensitive cloths or fabrics, and will protect the quality of your projects.

PRESSING HAMS

Pressing hams make ironing those hard-to-reach edges and curved seams and hems easier.

FOLDING PEN

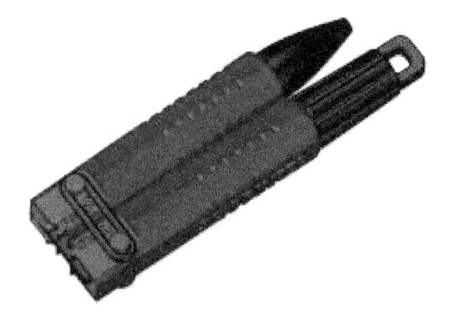

Folding pens make it easy to create precise folds in fabric. They also keep the folds sharp and in place so that you don't risk burning your fingers by trying to hold the hem in place while you iron.

Chapter 5:

Basic Sewing Patterns

Sewing stitches are so numerous, it's nearly impossible to list and catalogue them all. Most people, however, will find that just mastering a few of each type will give them all the skill they need to complete a wide number of different projects. Once you've learned these stitches, you can always go on to learn other, more decorative types once you get involved in a specific project or type of sewing.

Basting

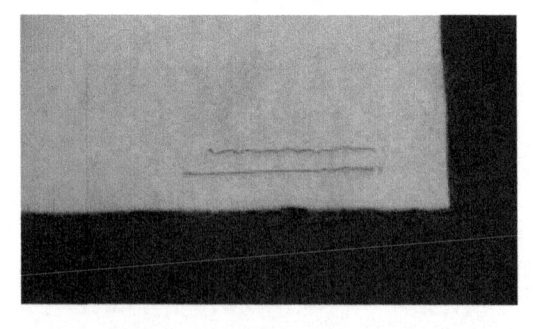

Basting is one of the easiest and simplest types of sewing. It's meant to temporarily join two pieces of fabric together so you can go back later and permanently stitch them together.

Basting is fast and can be done on the fly as well. If, for example, the hem of your skirt falls down at work, you can quickly baste it back into place, then fix it once you get home. Basting is used when you don't have pins to hold things together, and it is also used when making a quilt to hold your layers together before putting in the quilting stitches.

To baste:

- Gather up any size needle and thread.
- Thread the needle and knot the ends of the thread together.
- Place your two pieces of fabric together where they need to be joined.
- Push your needle through both pieces of fabric up from the bottom or underside so your knot doesn't show and pull the thread taut.
- Move down the fabric anywhere from 1/8 inch to 1 inch depending on how large you want your stitches to be and push the needle back through to the underside.
- Move the needle along the fabric about as much as you did for your first stitch (so if you used a 1-inch stitch, you'll move it along 1 inch on the underside and push it back up to the top), trying to keep your stitches in a straight line.
- Go forward another set amount and go back to the underside again.
- Continue until you reach the end of the fabric.

The basting stitch, when finished, will have evenly sized stitches and gaps moving along the fabric in a row. This will securely hold the fabric in place until you can make a more permanent stitch. The larger the stitches you make, the faster you'll go, but the less secure this will be. For example, if you're tacking up a hem, you may want to use smaller stitches to ensure it holds to the end of the day without snagging, but if you're quilting, you can use larger stitches because there will be so many of them, along with a quilting frame to hold everything in place.

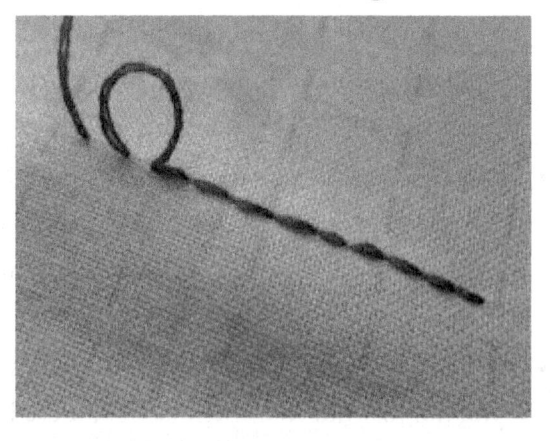

Back Stitching

If you've ever examined a hem that's been done on a sewing machine, you've seen an example of a back stitch, or a row of stitches that are all connected to one another with no spaces between them.

Back stitching is a more secure, permanent way to join two pieces of fabric together or to make a hem. Like basting, you can make your stitches larger or smaller depending on how quickly you want to work, and how long you need this stitch to last. The smaller the stitches, the less they will show and the longer they will hold – decades instead of years, for example. You can use any size of needle or thread to back stitch, but the smaller the needle, the smaller your stitches will be, and the easier time you'll have going through thick fabrics.

To back stitch:

- Thread your needle and tie off the ends.
- Position the pieces of cloth you intend to stitch. You may want to use pins or a basting stitch to hold them while you work because you'll be moving a lot more slowly, and you don't want your fabric to slip.
- Make a guide you can follow with your stitches to help keep them straight with chalk or a fabric pencil and a ruler. You'll stitch right on this mark so your finished stitch line will be even. Once you're done, wash the fabric and the mark will come out.
- Push your needle and thread up through the back of the fabric where the knot will not show. Pull the thread taut.
- Make a single stitch in the direction you want your row of stitches to go and push the needle and thread back to the underside of the fabric. This first

stitch should ideally be the size you want your finished stitches to be.

- Pull your thread taut on the underside of the fabric and move your needle down your mark about as far as your first stitch was. Push the needle up from the back and pull it tight. There will be a small gap between your first stitch and where your thread is now.
- Move your needle back to the end of the first stitch and push it back down to the underside at the same point where the first stitch ends. This will produce your second stitch, which will be connected to your first stitch.
- Repeat until you reach the end of the guide. This will give you a chain of connected stitches that will securely hold your fabric.

Keep in mind that the back stitch only produces a row of neat stitches on the top of the fabric. The underside will have longer, less connected stitches that aren't as neat or nice to look at. For this reason, only use the back stitch on items where the top is the only thing that shows.

Whip Stitch

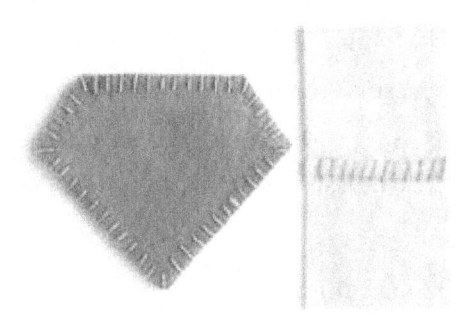

The whip stitch is another very fast stitch. It's typically used to close edges, such as an opening on a pillow, or to attach a hem without extremely visible stitches, such as in knit fabrics. It's a stronger, longer-lasting stitch than basting produces, so it's good for those times when you need to work quickly but need your work to hold.

The whip stitch is a round stitch, meaning that it produces a circular motion as you sew. If you're sewing two ends together, the stitch will be visible in a row of circular stitches across the top. If you're tacking up a hem, you'll see a row of vertical stitches on the back of the fabric, but only a tiny stitch every so often on the front.

To make the whip stitch:

- Thread your needle and knot the ends of the thread.
- Pin the edges of your fabric together where you want the stitches to be, leaving one end slightly open.

- Start your first stitch between the two layers of fabric, pushing your needle from the middle to the back. This will hide your knot between the two layers, since the whip stitch is often a visible one.
- Pull your thread taut on the back of the fabric, then pull it up toward the top of the two pieces you are joining.
- Wrap the thread over the top and push the needle back down right next to the first stitch, rather than on top of it. Your finished stitches will go at a slight angle rather than straight up and down.
- Repeat until you've completely joined the two pieces of fabric.

Like with the other stitches, you can vary your spacing between them, but the closer you can stitch, the tighter the fabric will hold together. If both sides of your fabric will be visible, try to keep the place where the thread goes in and out even. You can use a line drawn on the fabric if necessary, to make your stitches even.

Basic Cross-Stitch

While embroidery and cross-stitching are very different forms of sewing, you may want to start with cross-stitching before you move on to embroidery. Because of the way that cross-stitch projects follow a grid, you can more easily map out your design and get used to the larger needle and higher thread count than with a more freehand embroidery project.

When you start cross-stitching, you may want to begin with a special type of cloth called Aida. Aida is an inexpensive cloth that has a very pronounced grid. It's easier to use than linen, which makes it ideal for your first projects. Once you begin to get the hang of cross-stitching and you want to make something more ambitious, you can easily switch over to linen.

Unlike most other forms of sewing, cross-stitching requires additional tools beyond a needle and thread. Part of the process of cross-stitching is that the fabric needs to be pulled very taut as you push the needle through. To achieve this, you'll need to get a fabric hoop.

The fabric hoop is made up of two circles, often made of wood or metal. You'll put the fabric over the inner hoop and tighten the outer hoop around the edges. This will pull your fabric tight in the center and give you a very firm surface to stitch on.

Hoops come in all sizes. If you use a small one, you'll just need to reposition your fabric a few times over the course of the project. Large ones make it easier to work bigger sections of the design, but they can be a little cumbersome to hold.

Both cross-stitching and embroidery will use the same needles and a heavier thread known as floss. Embroidery floss comes in a skein of six threads twisted together to form one heavier thread. You can stitch with anywhere from one to six threads at a time, depending on how heavy you want the finished stitches to be. Some projects will specify the size of the needle and the number of threads, as well as the exact colors.

Most floss comes with a color number; you'll use this number to find the right colors for your project.

To make a basic cross-stitch:

- Thread your embroidery needle with the requisite number of threads and knot off the ends.
- Stretch a piece of fabric tightly between your hoops with the area on which you want to work toward the center.
- Locate the square you want to begin working in and find one corner of it from below.

- Push your needle up from below on your selected corner and pull your thread taut.
- Push your needle down again on the opposite diagonal corner on the same square. This will make a line cutting across the square, so the square will now resemble two triangles.
- Push your needle up from the bottom again on one of the empty corners of the same square. Pull your thread taut.
- Cross your initial stitch to go to the opposite diagonal corner and push your needle down again. Pull your thread taut.

This produces the basic X cross-stitch. You can continue to make X's across the area with the same color or vary your color per square to change the pattern. It is not uncommon to have multiple needles threaded with different colors so you can work a complex pattern quickly to get the design you want.

Chapter 6:

Getting Ready to Sew

You Are Ready to Sew!

If this is your first time with a machine, it will be somewhat daunting in the beginning. The best advice I can give you is to relax and have a lot of fun. You are not going to be turning out professional-looking garments the first time, so grab some old bits of material, something cheap that is not slippery – cotton or calico perhaps – and get some brightly colored thread. This is so you can see your stitches and monitor how well you are doing.

Threading Your Machine

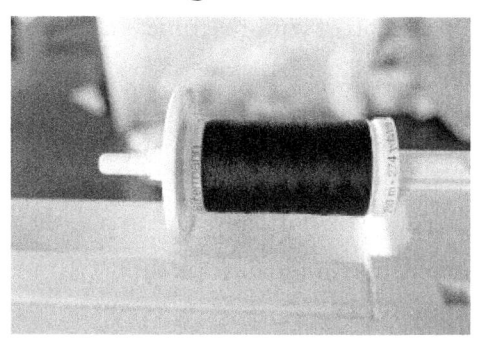

Before you begin working on any sort of project, you'll need to know how to thread your machine. I'll show you in pictures, but it'll be up to you to practice it several times. Every machine will be different, but to help you get a better understanding of how the process works, I can show you where the pictures about threading your machine will most likely be.

To start threading your machine, we'll start first with your thread. Place a spool of thread on the spindle at the top of your machine. Keep it in place by putting a spool holder over the top of it. A spool holder is a plastic cap that will fit snugly onto your spindle, clamping right over your spool. You can see it in the picture below; it looks like a little hat:

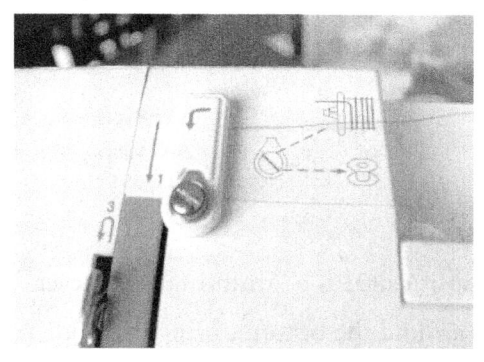

Take the thread off your spindle and get ready to start threading. On the top of your machine, you'll see a few images like the following picture:

Those images will be your machine's personal guide to threading your machine. Follow the guide. Once you have this portion figured out, you'll usually have to pull the thread down into the machine, like in the next picture:

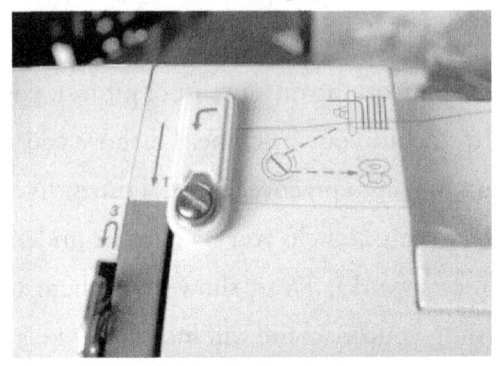

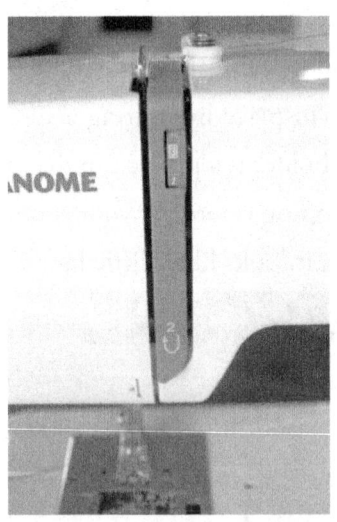

This loop is called the "thread take up lever." You'll loop your thread around the bottom, bringing it up. Your machine will have a metal piece that will take hold of the thread when you bring it up. Weave it through, and then the thread will come back down again. When you bring it down, you should use your machine's needle threader to help you get the string into the needle.

Your needle has been successfully threaded. But that's just the first part. In order to complete the threading, you'll need to put in your bobbin. Make sure it's been wound first, as in, the thread has been placed on it. You need a wound bobbin before you thread your machine. Next to your spindle for the spool, you'll see the following piece of metal:

This is the bobbin winder. Notice how the metal has space so it can be pushed to the right and then back to the left? When it's in the correct spot for winding bobbins, your machine will not sew, and pressing on the pedal will engage the bobbin winder.

To thread your bobbin, simply place your bobbin spool onto the metal pole. If you have fine eyesight, you should see in this picture a little piece of metal sticking out to the right of the bobbin winder. This metal will hold your bobbin in place.

Now, from your spool, take the free thread and wrap it around your bobbin a couple of times. I like to simply hold it while the bobbin spins, but many machines have a way to lock the loose thread into place, so you don't have to hold it. Do what works best for you. Once your thread has been securely attached to your bobbin, and the bobbin winder has been engaged by pushing the bobbin winder into the "on" position, use the foot pedal to wind that baby up!

Try not to go too fast though, or your bobbin will not thread evenly. You can help the threading along by gently pushing on the thread running from your spool to the bobbin if it begins to pile up in one place for too long without moving on.

Once your bobbin is nice and full, push the winder back into the "off" position. Remember, if your bobbin is "on," your machine will not sew, but the winder will move when the pedal is pressed.

Now you're ready to put your bobbin into place. To get the bobbin to your machine, take off the bobbin cover (usually a clear plastic almost-square piece). Reference the picture below:

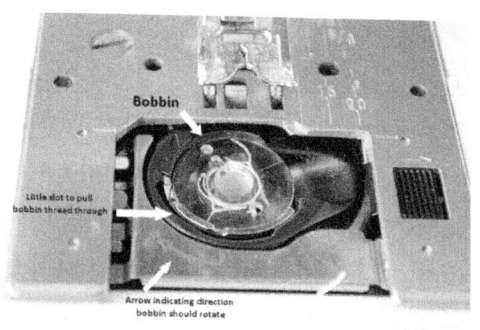

[Image: sewing machine bobbin area with labels "Bobbin", "Little slot to pull bobbin thread through", and "Arrow indicating direction bobbin should rotate"]

Your bobbin cover will fit right over this section of your machine, which is right beneath your footer. If your machine doesn't look anything like this, you'll need to consult your manual. Once your bobbin is in place, make sure you leave a piece of thread out, threaded through the thin slot. It is perfectly fine to leave the loose strand out while you work; in fact, it's necessary.

Put the cover back over your bobbin, and now you're ready to get sewing! Grab a piece of fabric (anything you can toss in the trash will do), pull up a chair with some back support, and read on to learn about sewing a straight line!

How to Prepare the Fabric

Now that you know the basic sewing stitches, you need to know how to prepare your fabric before you start sewing. There is more to sewing than just putting your thread and needle on the fabric. You need to avoid cutting through your fabric at once. You need to prepare your fabric so that you will be able to successfully make your sewing projects. Below are the things you need to do to prepare the fabric.

PRE-SHRINK THE FABRIC

When you buy a piece of fabric, make sure you know about the care instructions. These are usually found on the end of the fabric. Before sewing, it is important that all the elements of a particular project should be pre-shrunk, and this includes the zipper, interfacing and even the lining. To pre-shrink the fabric, fill a tub or basin with warm water and soak your fabric for a few seconds. Pre-shrinking the fabric ensures that the amount of fabric you use is just enough.

To find out if your fabric shrinks, cut a precise 2-inch square piece off your fabric and wet it with warm water. Press it with a steam iron. Draw a 2-inch square on a piece of paper and lay your dry fabric swatch over it. If it fills the entire box, then the fabric did not shrink. This test will save you a lot of time in figuring out whether your fabric will shrink or not.

If the fabric is colored, it may bleed a lot, so it is important to check for color fastness. To do this, you need to wash the fabric with a scrap of cotton fabric. If the white fabric comes out with a tint of color, then you can conclude that your fabric bleeds. You can control the bleeding of your fabric by washing it with three tablespoons of vinegar to help set the color. It is important that you set the colors on your fabric, especially if your project calls for two or three types of fabric. For fabrics that require dry-cleaning, you can steam shrink them by dampening the fabric and steam pressing it on the wrong side until it dries. Once it is dry, remove the creases from the fabric. Removing the creases ensures that the shapes as well as sizes of the pattern that you cut are accurate.

HOW TO CHECK THE GRAIN OF THE FABRIC

The grain refers to the direction in which the thread runs. When sewing different fabrics, it is important that the lengthwise and crosswise threads meet at the appropriate angles. If you sew on different threads, the final product will end up twisted or will hang crookedly.

It is important to take note that all types of woven fabrics have crosswise and lengthwise grains, and both run perpendicular to each other. If you are sewing a garment, the lengthwise grain should run vertically from the shoulders to the hem. If you are sewing drapes or curtains, you need to run the grain from top to bottom.

Prepare the Pattern

When sewing fabrics, you need to use patterns to be able to successfully create the final project. To prepare your fabric for pattern making, follow the steps below:

Give your pattern a press if it is folded or has wrinkles to help with accurate cutting.

Find a long table and wipe it down. Make sure it is free from any bumps that may obstruct you from laying out your pattern.

Fold your fabric in half lengthwise with all the right sides together, thus matching the two selvedges. Selvedges are the firmly woven border along the lengthwise edges. Folding the fabric makes it easier to cut it into two of the same piece at once. Before you fold the fabric, make sure the print is right side up.

Smooth the fabric to make the sides as flat as possible. If the fabric is longer than the table, lay out as much of it as you can while the other end is rolled neatly. By doing so, you can cut the pieces one at a time and unroll more as you go.

Place the pattern on top of the fabric. If you want to utilize all of your fabric, then you can arrange the fabric fold as long as the selvedges remain precisely parallel with one another.

Follow the pattern guide sheet so that you can determine where to put all the pattern pieces. Secure the patterns with pins and you are ready for cutting.

How to Cut the Fabric

Once you have prepared the pattern, it is time to cut through your garment. This procedure requires you to be accurate. It is very important for all seams to go together, and thus cutting with the grain is necessary. This section will provide you tips on how to cut fabrics properly so that you can sew better.

Use a cutting mat with a grid to help you cut your fabric precisely.

Make sure that you measure multiple spots on the entire grain line.

It is also important that all pattern pieces are laid correctly.

Place pins in the fabric. Leave a 1-inch allowance after the pattern. Place the pins within the allowance to secure the fabric in place.

Cut using very sharp scissors, as the seams of the hemline line up more easily if you use sharp scissors.

Cut along the allowance. If you feel like you cannot cut around the pins, use a rotary cutter instead. Using a rotary cutter can reduce the fraying of the edges of the fabric.

Selecting a Pattern

Ready-made patterns found in stores can be intimidating, but don't worry; you can learn to navigate them.

First of all, choose a pattern that is labeled "easy." Have a look at the front page. The sketch version of the garment will give you an idea of the front and back look.

Next, you will see the table of measurements on the back. Note that the measurements are usually smaller than ready-made garments you find in stores, so in order to avoid ending up with a garment that is too small, double check your body measurements and cut a little bit bigger than the pattern suggests.

You will see a list of pieces that you need to cut out. For example:
- Front
- Back
- Sleeve
- Pocket

Below that will be a list of items called "notions." Notions are any supplies other than fabric, such as buttons, lining, straps and threads.

Pattern layout

As you open the envelope, you will find all the pieces marked with their corresponding numbers. You will also see multiple dotted lines. These mark the different sizes, so make sure you cut the size that you need. Along these lines you will come across small triangles. These are notches that you will eventually need to cut out.

Cut out all the pieces in their biggest form.

Once you decide which size fits you, lay your fabric flat on an even surface. The fabric should lay straight, not diagonal. Next, pin the pattern pieces on the fabric. Cut out to the right size with long and firm cuts.

Here are the most common pattern markings and their functions:

```
1  ─────────        4  ─────────
                        ─ ─ ─ ─ ─

2  ─·─·─·─·─        5  ───  ┼  ┠──
   ─ ─ ─ ─ ─

3  ─────────        6  ✕    ⊙
```

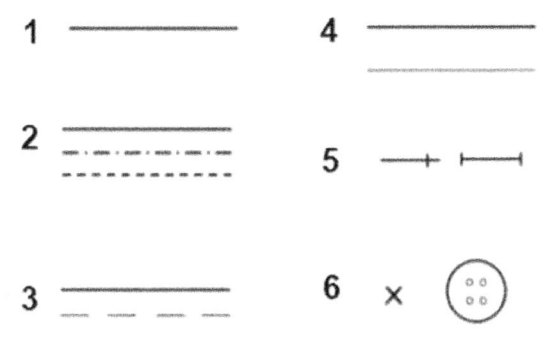

Cutting Line

Lines corresponding to different sizes
    Seam allowance
    Hem line
    Buttonholes
    Button placement

Marking

Once you have cut out your pieces, it is wise to mark important lines and points such as darts or buttonholes from the paper onto the fabric. One easy method is to use a fabric pen. Make a tiny hole in the paper to mark it onto the fabric. Another way is to make some hand stitches through the paper and fabric. Once you are done marking this way, you can gently tear off the paper. The stitches will remain in place on the fabric.

Sewing a Seam

There are four main seams that serve different purposes:

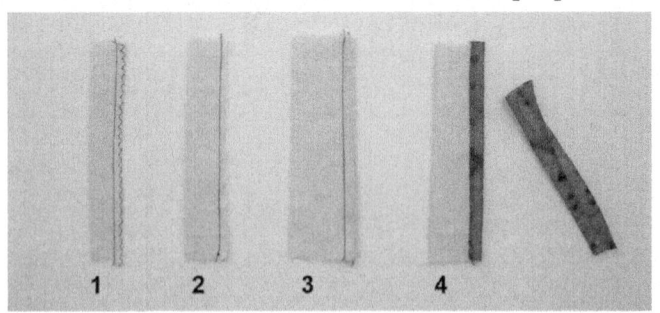

ZIGZAG SEAM

A zigzag seam is a good alternative to the serger seam. A serger or overlock machine is a separate machine that trims and finishes the raw edges of a garment while simultaneously sewing the pieces together. Sergers are usually more expensive than regular sewing machines, so unless you are very serious about sewing, the zigzag will do the job. After stitching the pieces together, set the machine on a zigzag stitch and sew along the edge.

STITCH AND PINK SEAM

Pinking shears are wonderful when it comes to finishing raw edges. The zigzag shape of the scissors prevents the fabric from fraying too much. This seam is suitable for most fabrics.

FRENCH SEAM

A French seam is suitable for delicate fabrics and classy outfits that should look good both on the right side as well as on the wrong side. For this seam, the seam allowance is twice as wide as a normal seam. The seam is stitched on the right side of the garment first, then turned inside out, pressed and stitched again.

HONG KONG SEAM

A more elaborate but elegant looking finish is done with a Hong Kong seam. Here, the edges are enclosed in bias tape. It is obviously more time consuming, but the results are well worth it. The Hong Kong seam gives a professional look and provides more structure due to its thickness.

Threading and Tension

Most sewing machines have a similar threading system. The correct threading is essential; otherwise the machine will not be able to stitch properly, or the thread might break while stitching.

The sewing machine may have markings to show you the steps you need to follow. First, place the thread spool onto the shaft.

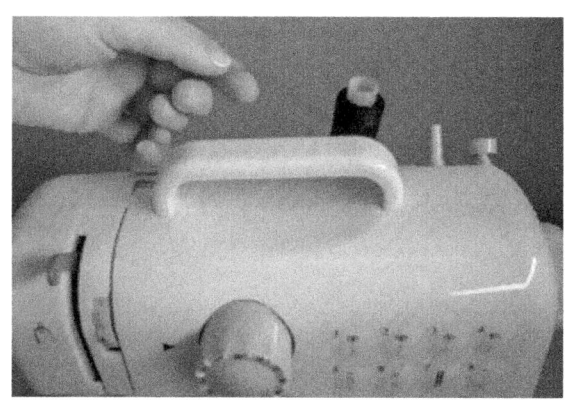

Then bring it along the marked areas.

Lastly, insert the thread through the needle. Some advanced sewing machines can do this with the push of a button.

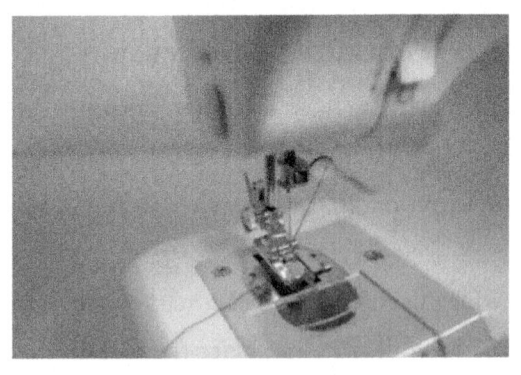

Threading the Bobbin

There are plastic bobbins and metal bobbins. Many sewing machines have a magnet in the bobbin hole to keep the metal bobbins in place. Test out whether your sewing machine has a magnetic bobbing hole by swiping a magnet or a small metal item on the area. Note that plastic bobbins are not as efficient on a magnetic bobbin hole.

SEWING EVEN A MONKEY CAN DO

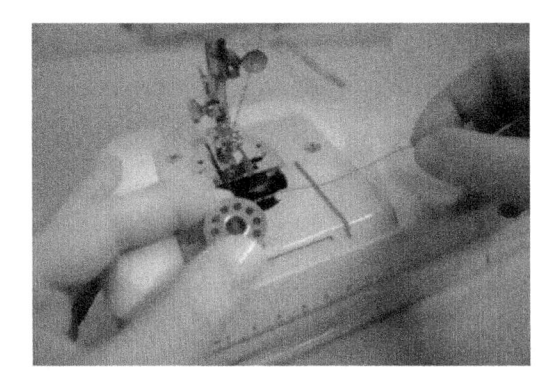

To get the thread out from the bottom onto the surface, align the bobbin with the thread unraveling clockwise. Let a few inches of thread stick out. Lower the needle by turning the wheel towards you. The needle will pull out the lower thread.

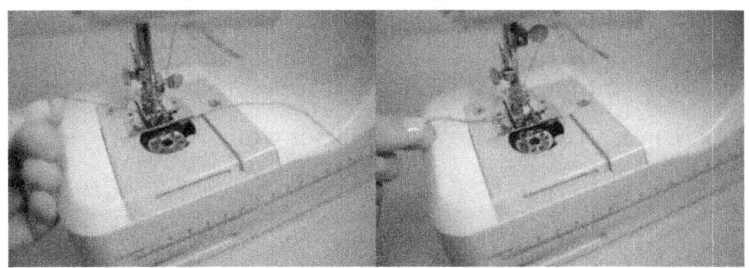

Bring the two threads underneath the presser foot, allowing a good 4" of thread to stick out. Then place your piece of fabric underneath and lower the foot.

Tension

Tension is the pulling strength between the upper and lower threads. There is a button or small wheel with which you can control the tension. In most cases you will use a tension of 3-4. The higher the number, the tighter the upper thread will be. For low tension, dial in a lower number.

The tension adjustment depends on what type of fabric you use. Every time you start using a new type of fabric, make a few stitches on a scrap to recalibrate the tension. Generally, the thicker the fabric, the higher the tension required.

SIGNS OF MISMATCHED TENSION

If the tension does not match the thickness of the fabric, the error will be obvious. Either the threads will be so tense that they gather the fabric, or the threads will be too loose and won't be able to keep the fabrics together. In other cases, the upper thread could simply snap because of high tension.

If this happens, simply dial the tension wheel forward or back and make some stitches until you find the right position. Knowing intuitively what tension you need requires some experience, so don't worry if you get it wrong.

Start Stitching

First, make sure your machine is set on basic stitch and you have threaded it properly. You should have around 4 inches of spare thread pulled out so that it can't unthread from the machine. Another thing that will help is if you hold the thread for the first couple of stitches.

Put the fabric underneath the presser foot, making sure the bit you want to stitch is at the front of the machine. Lower the presser foot to hold the fabric in place. This is an easy thing to forget, but you'll only do it a few times after your stitches run wild! Make it your mantra for a while – "lower the presser foot" – and keep on repeating it until you've mastered it.

The upper thread should be on top of the fabric but underneath the presser foot, while the lower thread from the bobbin should be underneath the fabric. Both of the threads should stick out to the back, so you are not sewing over them and getting them knotted up.

Before you begin any new line, check that you have lifted the needle up as high as it will go. This will help to prevent any of the frustrations of thread getting stuck or unraveling.

Turn on your machine. Lightly put both hands on the fabric on either side of the presser foot. This is to help guide it while sewing. Do not push or pull it, and keep your fingers out of the way of the needle – it will hurt! Lower your foot gently onto the pedal and start stitching.

Get lots of practice at this because it's the only way to learn how to guide the fabric and keep your stitching straight and neat.

Once you've got the hang of it, you can start looking at changing your speed. Most machines will have a speed setting button so you can slow it down or speed it up as you see fit. If your machine is one that does not have a speed setting, you will need to learn how to control speed through the pressure you put on the pedal.

How to Use the Hand Wheel

If you want to sew very slowly or you want to be able to move by just a stitch or two at a time for precision sewing, you can use the hand wheel. Turn it towards you to manually do what the pedal does. You can use the hand wheel to make your first stitch if you like to make sure the thread doesn't unravel or loosen and to ensure the needle goes where you want it. This is great for controlling the amount the needle moves through the fabric. I use it all the time for finishing off, turning corners, or for precision when doing topstitching.

CUT LOOSE

When you have finished your stitching, raise the presser foot so you can pull the fabric out slightly. Don't forget to raise your needle as well! You can do this with the hand wheel if you like; just raise the needle enough to make the thread give a little and you can move the fabric. Then, snip off the threads with small sharp scissors.

Some machines have a handy little blade on the side you can use to snip it off in one quick move, but you will need to check the manual for instructions on how to use it.

SECURING THE STITCHES

When you start sewing properly, i.e., not during a practice run, you will want to start securing your stitches so they can't come undone. There are two ways to do this:

Hold the reverse stitch lever on the machine so you sew backwards a few stitches over the end of the stitches – this is known as "back tacking." Stitch forwards again and snip the threads. This is probably the way you will do it most of the time.

If you have already sewn off the end of the fabric, simply tie the thread ends together into a double knot and snip off the ends. You would usually do this when you are sewing darts or in other tricky little spots where you don't want bulky reverse stitching.

STITCHING A STRAIGHT LINE

Once you have the hang of stitching with the machine, it is time to start learning how to stitch in a straight line. To begin, use a ruler and draw a straight line on the fabric. You can use the needle plate guidelines as well – these will tell you how far the needle is from the edge of the fabric. Take some time to learn how the fabric goes through the machine and how to control it until you are satisfied that you can sew in a straight line.

STITCHING A CURVED LINE

When you can sew in a straight line, have a go at sewing in curves. Again, draw a line on your fabric, a nice wavy one, but keep the curves large for now until you have the hang of it. Put the fabric onto the machine and make sure the presser foot is in line with the first part of the curve.

When you start to sew, gently guide the fabric with your hands and make sure the presser foot remains in line with the upcoming curve. Go slowly; stop as many times as you need to keep up with the curves. This will take practice, so keep going until you are certain your stitching is following the line of your curves.

One thing you might find with curves is that you need to snip the fabric to keep these curves nice and flat. If you are sewing a curved seam, for example, when you turn the item the right way out, there may be areas that are puckered. Snipping the fabric will prevent this from happening.

TURNING THE CORNER

Start by drawing a right angle on your fabric. Get the fabric into the machine and start stitching along the line until you get to the corner. At the point of the corner, the needle must be pushed down through your fabric – if it isn't going, use the hand wheel to help it. Raise the presser foot when the needle is in the right place, turn the fabric so the next straight line is in front of you and check that it is parallel to the needle plate guidelines. Put the presser foot back down and continue stitching.

Chapter 7:

Taking Accurate Measurements

Taking accurate measurements is also essential when it comes to sewing so that you don't waste time, effort, and of course, needles, thread and fabric. This chapter will provide you with a quick guide about the proper measurements of garments and pillow covers, as well as how to correctly take body measurements for clothing. Check out the guidelines below.

Preparations before Sewing

<u>FABRIC LAYOUT</u>
Before laying out your fabric, make sure that you have plenty of space to work, like a large table with appropriate height. Height does matter a lot since a good height will be more suitable for your back.

A sewing table can be roped in, as its height is higher than that of a normal table. Since the job of sewing requires a lot of attention at the minutest levels, doing it on the floor will lead to a sore back and painful leg muscles.

Every important element must be assembled beforehand, like pattern pieces, layout instruction, pins, scissors and fabric.

Some important issues related to the laying of the fabric are as follows:

STRETCHING IT BACK INTO SHAPE

Take your fabric and fold it in the same fashion as shown in your pattern instruction before laying it on a cutting surface. At times, if you don't get your fabric nicely laid in line on the surface, it may be a bit stretched out of shape. If such is the case, try stretching the fabric slightly along the diagonal.

With the help of another person, stretch the fabric from one corner to the opposite corner in the same direction in which it requires adjustment. Another option to counter this problem is pre-washing, which is just as effective a solution.

STRETCH OF FABRIC VS. GRAIN

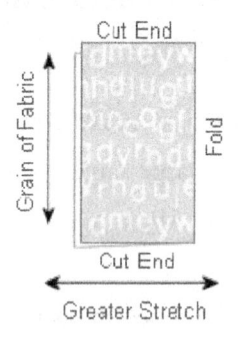

Cut End

Grain of Fabric | *Fold*

Cut End

Greater Stretch

Following the layout according to the correct direction is extremely important. Different fabrics have different directions for stretching; for example, you may want to stretch across the back of a skirt.

FABRIC CUTTING

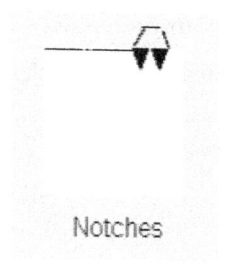

Notches

Before you start with the cutting process, it is necessary to position all the pieces in the correct order. This also ensures that you have a complete understanding of the layout and there is enough space available to work upon all the pieces. If you are a beginner, it is better to stick to the layout instructions as given, following them in letter and spirit. Once you start gaining experience, you may have your own way of laying out the pieces.

After this is done, you must secure your pattern in the right place before starting off with the cutting procedure. For this you'll need pins and weights. Of the two, pins are more useful and precise, as they do not pose the risk of being knocked out of place.

As regards the rotary cutter, it may be a good option but is quite difficult to use around the corners as it easily overshoots your mark; moreover, it is very sharp and might not be safe for a beginner. Scissors serve your purpose well until you get more experience.

MARKING PIECES

There are numerous ways to mark the fabric, which you can choose depending on your preferences and the type of fabric in use. Some of the common marking elements are:

Tailor Tack

Pillow Cover Measurements

Pillow covers are some of the easiest and most affordable sewing projects you can undertake. Here's a list of various types of pillows and their corresponding measurements.

STANDARD PILLOWS

Dimensions: 20 x 26 inches
   Amount of Fabric Needed: 5/8 yard

SQUARE PILLOWS

There are different dimensions for these, as you can see below:
   30 x 30 inches – 1 yard
   20 x 20 inches – ¾ yard
   18 x 18 inches – 5/8 yard
   16 x 16 inches – ½ yard
   14 x 14 inches – ½ yard
   12 x 12 inches – 1/3 yard

QUEEN SIZE PILLOWS

Dimensions: 20 x 30 inches
   Amount of Fabric Needed: 1 and 1/8 yards

KING SIZE PILLOWS

Dimensions: 20 x 36 inches
   Amount of Fabric Needed: 1 and 1/8 yards

Garment Measurements

Taking measurements for garments can be tricky because of the wide variety of both sizes and types of clothing. But it's good to have a guide to give you an idea of estimated measurements that could work for different body types, like the one below.

LONG SLEEVED DRESS WITH SKIRT

    35 to 36 inches – 5 yards
    44 to 45 inches – 3 and 5/8 yards
    50 inches – 3 and ¼ yards
    52 to 54 inches – 3 and 1/8 yards
    56 to 60 inches – 3 yards

SHORT SLEEVED DRESS WITH STRAIGHT SKIRT

    35 to 36 inches – 4 and ¼ yards
    44 to 45 inches – 3 and 1/8 yards
    50 inches – 2 and ¾ yards
    52 to 54 inches – 2 and 5/8 yards
    56 to 60 inches – 2 and 3/8 yards

BIAS CUT CAMISOLE

    35 to 36 inches – 1 and 1/3 yards
    44 to 45 inches – 1 and 1/3 yards
    50 inches – 1 and ¼ yards
    52 to 54 inches – 1 and 1/8 yards
    56 to 60 inches – 1 yard

CAP-SLEEVED BLOUSE

    35 to 36 inches – 1 and 1/3 yards
    44 to 45 inches – 1 and 1/3 yards
    50 inches – 1 and ¼ yards
    52 to 54 inches – 1 and 1/8 yards
    56 to 60 inches – 1 yard

LONG SLEEVED BLOUSE WITH TIE

    35 to 36 inches – 3 and ¾ yards
    44 to 45 inches – 2 and 7/8 yards
    50 inches – 2 and 5/8 yards
    52 to 54 inches – 2 and 3/8 yards
    56 to 60 inches – 2 and ¼ yards

LONG SLEEVED SHIRT/BLOUSE

    35 to 36 inches – 2 and ½ yards
    44 to 45 inches – 2 and 1/8 yards
    50 inches – 1 and ¾ yards
    52 to 54 inches – 1 and ¾ yards
    56 to 60 inches – 1 and 5/8 yards

SHORT SLEEVED SHIRT/BLOUSE
    35 to 36 inches – 2 yards
    44 to 45 inches – 1 and 5/8 yards
    50 inches – 1 and ½ yards
    52 to 54 inches – 1 and 3/8 yards
    56 to 60 inches – 1 and ¼ yards

SOFTLY GATHERED SKIRT
    35 to 36 inches – 2 and ¼ yards
    44 to 45 inches – 1 and ¾ yards
    50 inches – 1 and 5/8 yards
    52 to 54 inches – 1 and ½ yards
    56 to 60 inches – 1 and 3/8 yards

A-LINE SKIRT
    35 to 36 inches – 2 and ¼ yards
    44 to 45 inches – 1 and ¾ yards
    50 inches – 1 and 5/8 yards
    52 to 54 inches – 1 and ½ yards
    56 to 60 inches – 1 and 3/8 yards

STRAIGHT SKIRT
    35 to 36 inches – 2 yards
    44 to 45 inches – 1 and 5/8 yards
    50 inches – 1 and ½ yards
    52 to 54 inches – 1 and 3/8 yards
    56 to 60 inches – 1 and ¼ yards

BERMUDA SHORTS

    35 to 36 inches – 2 and ½ yards
    44 to 45 inches – 2 and 1/8 yards
    50 inches – 1 and 7/8 yards
    52 to 54 inches – 1 and ¾ yards
    56 to 60 inches – 1 and ¼ yards

CAPRI PANTS

    35 to 36 inches – 2 and ¾ yards
    44 to 45 inches – 2 and ¼ yards
    50 inches – 2 and 1/8 yards
    52 to 54 inches – 2 yards
    56 to 60 inches – 1 and ½ yards

FULL LENGTH PANTS

    35 to 36 inches – 3 and ¼ yards
    44 to 45 inches – 2 and 5/8 yards
    50 inches – 2 and 5/8 yards
    52 to 54 inches – 2 and ¼ yards
    56 to 60 inches – 2 and ¼ yards

How to Take Accurate Body Measurements

Basically, you need to take the following six measurements:

HEIGHT
Stand barefoot with your back to a flat wall.

BUST
Measure at the fullest part of the chest, making sure to keep the tape snug and even as you wrap it around the back. Your arms should be at your sides while you are being measured.

WAIST
Measure at the natural waist (the narrowest part of the torso). Tie a string or ribbon at the natural waist and keep in place for measurement #5.

HIGH BUST
Lay the tape just above the bust and wrap it under the arms and straight across the back.

HIP

Wrap the tape measure around the widest part of the hips, or at least 7 inches below the waistline.

Notes:

Make sure that the torso and the floor are perpendicular to each other as you measure the subject.

Measure the subject while he/she is only in his/her underwear or wearing a leotard for more accurate measurements.

Don't try to take your own measurements. This will only yield inaccurate results.

Chapter 8:

Common Mistakes Sewing Beginners Make

Being a beginner in anything is not always easy, and mistakes are made from time to time. If you have already made a few mistakes, there is no need to worry because this is the way you will learn and have an easier time in the future. Here is a list of some of the common mistakes that tailors make in the beginning. Knowing these mistakes will help you avoid them for an easier start:

Starting on a really expensive sewing machine

There is a common belief that the most expensive sewing machines are the best ones to use because they have more features and they are much easier to handle than other machines. This is not really true, especially for beginners. A beginner needs to start on a simple sewing machine that can meet his/her needs for learning and starting on the first projects, and then maybe you can get a better sewing machine once you have mastered a few complex techniques that require the use of the most advanced machines. Besides, an expensive sewing machine does not mean that it is the best in the market. What you should have in mind at all times is the quality of the machine and your current needs. It is very easy to get a good sewing machine to get you started in sewing without spending so much money on it.

Using the wrong tools on a project

Many people do not take time to gather all the tools they need to get started in sewing and they start looking for other tools they can use in the place of the actual tools. This is a mistake that can make you mess up your first projects, and this can kill your motivation to sew. The problem is that actual tools for sewing are meant to make things easy for you and to help you work faster. In your effort to save money on the right sewing tools, you end up compromising on time and effort. In the end, you will not enjoy sewing as much since you are taking longer on projects than you should and maybe you keep making endless mistakes. To avoid all this frustration, invest some money on good sewing tools.

Working on more than one project at a go

This is a very common mistake with many tailors, not just beginners. Expert tailors are probably able to handle more than one project at a go, but a beginner may not be. Beginners are moved by the excitement to start sewing and to learn a lot of things at the same time, and this is what can easily push you to take more than one project at a time. The best thing to do for a beginner is to start on one project, finish it and then move to the next one.

The reason for this is because there is always something new to learn from your first project. You'll learn some skills and techniques and you'll also learn from some mistakes, which can help you make things better on your second project. Again, once you finish the first project, you can be sure that you will always finish other projects in the future.

Buying patterns that have to be altered

Sewing beginners are always looking for things to try out, and sometimes you might be lured into buying patterns that will require major alterations. This is not a big deal for experienced tailors because they can alter any pattern perfectly, but for a beginner, this can be frustrating, time consuming and discouraging. The last thing you need is to spend so much time on a project that will not turn out the way it should just because you cannot make the alterations right. Beginners learn better when they start on simple projects; then they can advance slowly instead of taking major projects when they are still learning the basics.

Buying a lot of things before getting started

This is also a result of the excitement to get started. Many people buy a lot of fabric, patterns and even notions before they can even start on their first project. These will overwhelm you so much and push you so hard to sew things that you have not even learned how to sew. You need to take a step at a time in sewing. Even if things are on sale, you need to know that they will be on sale again in the future, probably at a time when you need them. Relax and only buy what you need at that instant. Once you learn a new skill, buy the fabric you need and work on it. This will also save on space and ensure that you are an organized tailor from the word go.

Downloading complex patterns with no guide

These days there are many sewing patterns that you can download from the internet in PDF format, and they can help you so much in making great designs. The problem comes when you download too many patterns with no guide. This means you will need to figure things out yourself, which is time consuming and frustrating. You will find very good patterns that you cannot even design because you do not know how to go about it. This is not good for a beginner; you need to download patterns that come with instructions so that you will save on time, and also for fast learning.

Not taking time to learn a sewing machine

This is a basic tool that you will use all the time; therefore, it should be the first thing you master, even before you learn the first sewing skill. You need to take time to learn how to thread, for instance. Practice a few times so that you can always thread when need be without wasting so much time on it. Learn everything about your machine beforehand, including all the features and how they work. This will help you save a lot of time when you start sewing.

Ignoring fabric suggestions on patterns

Every pattern will come with fabric suggestions. There are specific kinds of fabrics that are good for certain patterns. You need to understand this so that you will not make a mistake that can ruin your project in the end. Working with the right fabric at all times contributes so much to the success of sewing projects.

Chapter 9:

Using Your Machine's Stitch Functions

Most machines come with cool functions that create incredible stitch designs. We're going to talk about the zigzag stitch.

It's a very sturdy stitch. When you're looking for something to hold extra tight, the zigzag is your stitch to choose.

This stitch can also prevent fraying. Have you ever dealt with fraying? There's nothing more frustrating than a perfectly good project fighting frays. Keep them at bay with this sturdy stitch.

This third reason is probably the most common reason for teaching you the zigzag: it's commonly used with buttonholes and appliqué designs. Appliqué designs are "add-ons" to your sewing project. Think a set of crazy eyes, felt, or a cute little fabric owl that you want to sew onto a baby onesie. The best stitch to use is the zigzag.

So, let's get started! Sewing this stitch, you'll see, is really as easy as pressing a button – literally! You're going to start the exact same way you did with the straight stitch. Make sure your machine is properly threaded with bobbin in place.

To access the zigzag function, you'll have to review your machine's manual to learn how to switch stitches. You can actually lengthen the width and length of the stitch, but right now, we're going to keep things average. You can adjust the length using this wheel:

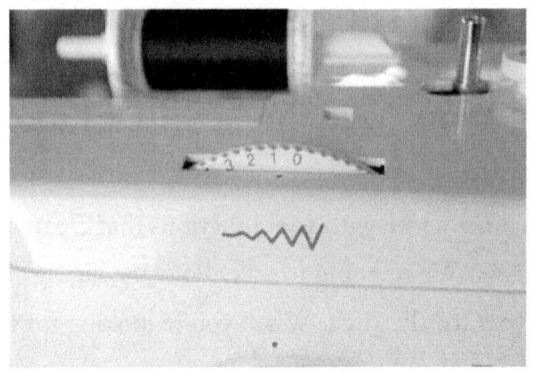

This spinning wheel is usually located along the top of your machine. How it is marked varies from machine to machine. For this zigzag stitch, you'll want to play around with how the length will make your stitches look. The first image is a basic zigzag stitch of average length:

This next image of the stitch has the LENGTH turned down as low as it can go. See how you can barely make out the zigzag?

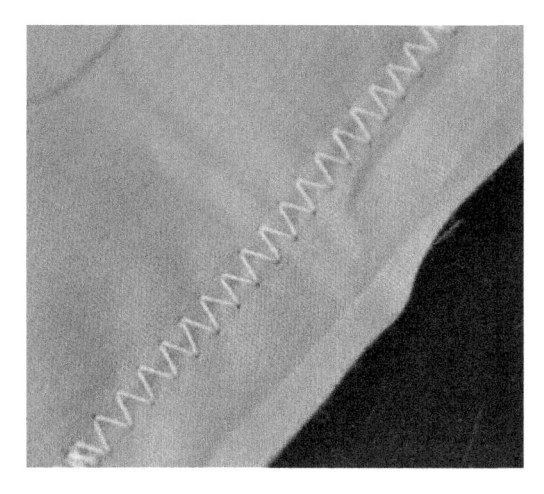

The following image has the LENGTH and the WIDTH adjusted, making the total zigzag a little smaller than the basic stitch.

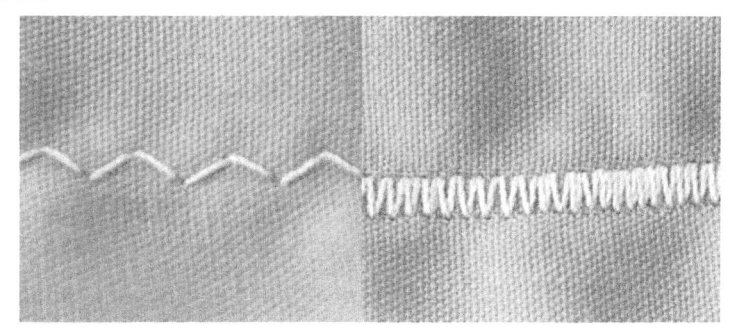

The LENGTH in the image below has been adjusted to make the stitches very long and further apart.

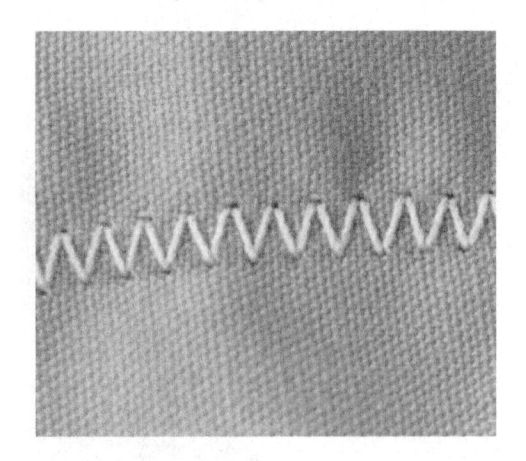

You'll have to play around with your machine to really get the hang of how to adjust these settings to pull off the type of stitch you're looking for in your next project. Now let's get ready to sew!

Remember to lower the presser foot down onto the fabric to keep it in place. Now lower your needle into the fabric. Double check to make sure your machine has the zigzag stitch selected and start sewing. Remember to start off slow, and only sew forward about an inch. Afterwards, press your reverse button to go back over your work. Now sew forward again to complete the knot and keep forward.

For now, just use the edge of your presser foot, or try using one of the seam allowance guides, to help you sew straight.

While you're sewing, you might notice that the stitch creates a tunnel beneath it. This usually happens with lightweight fabric. To get around this, find the stitch on your machine that looks like a zigzag, but with dotted lines. In the picture I used previously, it was marked with a letter "D." This dotted zigzag will give three stitches per zig and per zag, which greatly reduces the tunneling effect. Go ahead and give it a try! While you can complete most basic sewing projects with the zigzag stitch and the straight stitch, grab a piece of fabric and test out the other stitches just for fun. Your manual probably has the names of the stitches listed, so you can easily look up projects containing them if you're curious!

Chapter 10:

The Special Techniques of Sewing

In the last section we made an effort to teach all beginners the basics of seaming and stitching in a way they can easily understand. But for a learner, this is not enough. One needs to move forward to enhance one's skill, towards the special techniques of sewing and stitching.

Hemming

Hemming is needed at the end of trousers, necklines and sleeves. Moreover, the raveling of fabric can be avoided by making beautiful hemming. The following are the major steps of hemming:

Turn around your fabric to an appropriate seam allowance. In most cases, a turn of ¼ inch will be enough. Now, when you have turned the edge equally, you need to press the fabric over the turn. It will give the fabric a settled and pressed look.

Pin up the folded portion in a way so that the fabric settles in your hand. Moreover, if you add too many pins, it will eventually disturb your sewing, so you need to make an accurate adjustment in this regard. Now stitch at the pressed folds.

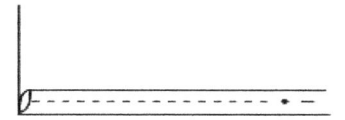

There may be cases when you will need softer hems. In all these instances, you will make your hem by hand using a needle and thread.

Use of two threads to create a gathering

The gathering technique in sewing is basically used for all those accessories and dresses which need a little ruffle. It creates marvelous fullness in skirts, sleeves and hats. But the gathering technique needs some extra fabric in order to be applied, so if your plan is to go for gathering, you must plan it ahead so that you are equipped with all the necessary items and fabrics well before time. Gathering can be either light or intense, and in both these cases the quantity of fabric needed will vary.

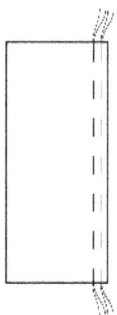

The first step of the gathering technique is to have a correct seam allowance. One thing which people usually forget is a double seam allowance, as there will be a double seam for gathering, so you need to keep your seam allowance double what it is normally.

Another technique used in gathering is known as basting. For that, you need to keep your stitch length as long as possible.

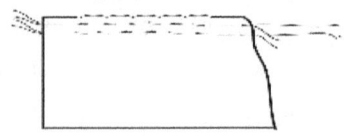

Now make the first seam along the length of the cloth at a width of ¼ inches. When you are completed with the first seam, make another seam at a distance of ¼ inches. Now you have two consecutive seams. Be careful not to cut off the threads at the end of each seam; these threads will be used to create the gathers.

When done with the seams, gently pull off the thread from one end by keeping a hand on the other. Gentle pulling will enable the gathering to be created. Now adjust the gathering in such a way that the gathers are adjusted evenly on the fabric.

Another technique is to pull the threads from both ends so that you can get more saturated gathers.

Appliqué work

This is a very beautiful pattern-making technique which can add a decorative touch to your dress or any other accessory.

Cut the shape of the fabric into different designs. These will be the designs appearing as the pattern on another piece of fabric, so cut the shape very carefully.

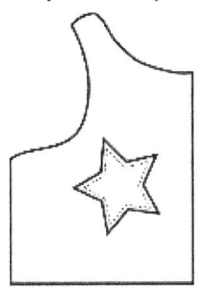

Now put the cut piece on the fabric on which you want to paste the desired shape. The market is full of different products which can help you to stick the cut piece to the fabric. One such product is called fusible web.

Use a zigzag stitch in order to keep it firm and put the pattern in place. Stitch around the corners and alongside the edges so that the shape cannot get distorted. One trick here is to keep the zigzag stitch only on the piece placed on the fabric. Do not stitch your underneath fabric.

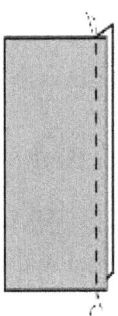

French seam

French seams are another beautiful style for making your dress extremely stylish. French seams will prevent any kind of raveling of the fabric.

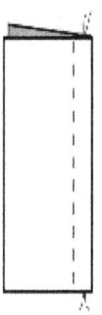

First of all, turn your fabric to the wrong side and stitch it to the end.

Now turn it right side out and make another stitch to the end of the fabric. Make sure the second seam is apart from the first seam and it makes use of the distance left between.

These are a few of the techniques which are largely used in a number of different sewing projects. Although these have been provided with a step by step approach, you can also make your own innovative styles through a trial and error method.

Flat-felled seams

These seams are common in men's wear. Their main purpose is to add a clean and professional look to the final product, whether you are sewing shirts, sportswear or other garments. This is a strong, durable seam, and it will give your garment more structure without requiring you to add more bulk to the garment.

This is how it is done: one edge is folded over the edge of the other raw end, and then it is top stitched down flat.

This kind of seam will work perfectly on reversible garments that are meant to look the same on both sides. If you are sewing a garment with tight curves, you should not use these seams.

Bias bound seams

Bias seams are also called the Hong Kong seam finish. They are basically an easy way you can add a level of expertise to a garment you are sewing. This is a great way to add some color to your projects in order to make them more appealing.

The raw edge of the fabric is encased completely in a strip of bias tape, which leaves a clean look on the inside of your garment.

This seam will not be easy, but learning it will be of great benefit since you can always add something beautiful to your projects to make them more appealing. This technique is best used on heavy garments or those garments that do not have a lining.

Using a rotary cutter

Every tailor will need a rotary cutter and a cutting mat. However, you have to learn the skill of cutting with a rotary cutter to be able to use these invaluable tools effectively. A rotary cutter will help you cut out patterns more easily and accurately, at faster speed. The cutting mat will protect your work surface from unnecessary cuts.

The rotary cutter should always be kept sharp; therefore, you might have to keep a stock of rotary blades so that you can change them out when one begins to get dull.

Princess seams

These are basically a variation of darts that are used to create rounded curves that give shape to women's clothing. What you achieve through princess seams is an elongated, slimming appearance that should be tailored with the wearer in mind. These kinds of seams are perfect for fitted dresses and jackets in order to bring out a snugly contoured bust and waist. They are common in bridal gowns and couture dresses, although they are slowly gaining popularity in most women's dresses.

There are a variety of other decorative seams available in most modern sewing machines that you can use in order to bring the best out of every project you work on.

Pressing and ironing

Ironing is an important part of sewing as it helps to remove any wrinkles on a garment you are working on. Ironing is very different from pressing; although both of them use an iron box, pressing is the recommended technique in sewing. Ironing, which involves gliding the iron back and forth over the garment, can be damaging to the garment, which is why pressing is more recommended for sewn garments. Pressing involves placing the iron on the fabric and leaving it there for just a few seconds, then removing it. Pressing will not distort the fibers of your garment or fabric, and it will help to set and blend your stitches to get a nice, crispy seam thereafter. You should always take proper care of your fabric or garment when pressing.

Clipping corners and curves

This is a very simple but important technique that can help a lot when you are sewing. Seaming projects that have corners and curves are not easy, and on such projects, you have to fight hard to keep the garment in place at all times. Clipping corners and curves can help make the work easier for you.

Clipping a corner at a diagonal, close to the seam but not too close, will get you a nice and easy corner to work on, and it will be perfect when you turn your project right side out.

Do the same for curves as well. Those curves that look like mountains can be notched and those that look like valleys can be clipped for ease of work and a perfect finish.

Stay stitching

This is a technique that will help you prevent any kind of distortion on your curves. Stay stitching is done on a curve, and it entails setting your stitch length to say 1.5, then starting your stitching 1/8 inch in from your stitching line.

Curves should be stay stitched immediately after they are cut in order to avoid distortion because moving your fabric a few times after cutting is enough to mess up your curve.

Fussy cutting

This is a technique you can use on a patterned fabric in order to isolate a motif. This is a much easier way to create easy appliqués that will be added to garments or projects that are meant for home décor.

In order to get the best cut, cut roughly around the motif you want to isolate, ensuring that enough room is left out around the edges. Then trim the motif to its actual size, leaving out a small seam allowance. Now you can place the motif on the fabric, and to keep it in place, you can use satin stitches around it or use a spray adhesive.

Use of bar tracks

Bar tracks are used to reinforce areas that could receive a lot of stress once the project is done, such as pocket openings. Without the reinforcement, these areas will get weaker by the day, and this can damage the garment. Bar tracks can be done with your sewing machine using a zigzag stitch, or you can sew it by hand using whip stitch.

Chapter 11:

Machine Maintenance

Procedure of Sewing Machine Maintenance

Servicing your sewing machine is a simple task but requires precision. The steps to perform proper and effective maintenance are as follows.

Removing dust is one of the biggest causes of jams and breakdowns in sewing machines of any model. That is why the first thing you must remove is dust.

To do this, you'll need a brush and a soft bristle brush.

On many occasions, dust accumulates and mixes with oil residues, forming lint layers that are difficult to remove. So, you must have patience, perseverance and time available to remove all this dirt.

Some important parts from which you must remove dust are:

Needle holder

Reel holder

Bobbin cases

Presser foot

Inside of the bobbin case

In addition, all the parts we can access, and anywhere we notice dust, must be well cleaned.

The inner part, not only external parts, requires in-depth maintenance. Also, the inside of the sewing machine requires special treatment to guarantee its operation.

To do this, we must dismantle the presser foot and the shuttle to reach inaccessible corners.

If your machine uses a metal coil, you must disassemble it and dust it off. You should also remove the coil and check that it does not have dust or other harmful residues.

Once you have made sure there is no dust inside the most important parts of the machine, you will proceed to greasing. Greasing your sewing machine will allow the most important moving parts to run smoothly.

You should know that you cannot apply oil to all the pieces that come to mind. In fact, the main piece to be oiled is the bobbin case.

You can also put oil on the shuttle and on the needle bars. This will be enough to guarantee good moving parts mechanics.

It is not necessary to put a large amount of oil on the parts previously described. One drop on each piece is more than enough.

Assemble and test. When you finish cleaning and oiling your sewing machine, it is recommended that you try it immediately. This ensures that all parts have been put in place correctly.

It also serves to let you feel the difference in performance so that you can compare how it worked without proper maintenance and how it works after maintenance.

In the following pages you can see how to maintain your sewing machine at home, quickly and easily.

Accessories Required for Maintenance

As you have noticed, the maintenance of sewing machines is relatively simple. However, the effectiveness can be diminished if you do not use the correct materials and products. Here is a list of the recommended products and accessories for this process:

Nylon Cleaning Brush Set: For a deep and effective cleaning, it is necessary to use brushes with tiny and flexible bristles. That is why we recommend the ZOEON brush set.

The set contains 10 brushes, each 21 centimeters long, but with different styles on the tips.

These are ideal for reaching the most difficult-to-reach places on sewing machines. In addition, they can be used to clean other appliances with similar characteristics.

5-pc. Double Pointed Sewing Machine Brushes: This brush incorporates a double pointed structure in its design. This allows cleaning with different shades of firmness.

The pack is made up of 5 brushes with the same characteristics. When one of the brushes deteriorates, you will have a substitute immediately.

Sewing machine oil, 100 ml: Another essential product for the maintenance of sewing machines is oil. This allows the lubrication of the moving parts, lengthening the useful life of the machine components.

We recommend using Alfa sewing machine oil. Its 100 ml package is ideal for easy transport and use.

This oil provides a protective coating to sewing machine parts that prevents corrosion and dust from damaging components.

The cap is designed to easily add oil at key locations on the sewing machine.

5-liter sewing machine oil: If you own a large company with many sewing machines, you will likely require a large amount of oil. For these cases, we recommend 5-liter sewing machine oil.

It is an oil designed for the maintenance of domestic machines and also for industrial models. It is resistant to high temperatures, forming a durable and effective film.

Chapter 12:

Troubleshooting Common Sewing Problems

Can you repair your sewing machine if it encounters minor problems?

Here's a guide to troubleshooting the most common sewing issues faced by beginners:

BREAKING NEEDLES

Always start with a straight new needle when beginning a new project. Take care to avoid bent needles, as it can lead to the needle breaking and entering your eye! If your needles are breaking now you know where to look first!

NOT-THREADING

The primary cause might be that your spool is not properly chained through the thread guide. When starting to sew, make sure your thread guide is up.

Are your stitches opening up at the ends?

Always take care to double-stitch the edges. To do this, pull the fabric back and forth after finishing the straight stitch and stitch again on the edge of the fabric, respectively.

UNPROFESSIONAL SEAMS

For a perfect seam, never remove the fabric when done with a straight stitch. While you change the direction, leave the needle pivoted down on the fabric and continue stitching.

UNDUE NOISE WHEN ACTIVE

Something is jammed in your machine. De-assemble and clean the lint off your machine with a brush.

Grandma's Sewing Hacks

Never leave your thread guide down when starting to sew; otherwise, your needle will unthread the moment you start sewing.

Always start by checking the stitches on a rough patch of fabric before starting on a brand-new fabric.

Avoid using oddly shaped needles, as there is a chance they will ruin your eyes as well as the work, irreparably!

If you notice any skipped stitches, your needle is rotten!

Always keep a patch of the fabric and 2 inches of thread from the material you work on, as a thumbnail record of your accomplishments.

If you notice any strange noises coming from your sewing machine, immediately unplug it and call the manufacturer.

Just like your computer, there is a manual restart to troubleshoot your sewing machine. Re-threading and re-winding the bobbins from square one will help you to remove mild jams.

Chapter 13:

10 Sewing Projects

Oven Gloves

Make these cheerful oven gloves with an eye-catching heart motif, or one of your own designs, in a color scheme to match your kitchen décor. In this project you will learn about wadding and interfacing and how to enhance any sewing project by the addition of your own appliqué designs.

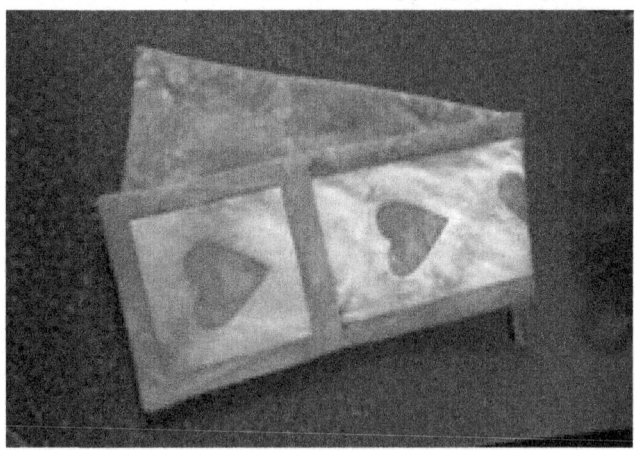

You Will Need:

- 2 x fat quarters in main color

- 2 x fat quarters in a contrast color (bear in mind that this fabric will be used for the heart motifs)
- 2 x 35" x 8-½" (89 cm x 43 cm) pieces of pure cotton batting (wadding)
- 2 x 8-½" (21 cm) squares of medium-weight iron-on interfacing
- ¼ yard (25 cm) fusible web
- Small piece of contrast fabric for hanging loop
- All-purpose polyester thread in a toning color
- A strong cotton fabric is recommended for these oven gloves.

Too Hot to Handle?

I recommend you use pure cotton fabrics and wadding for this project. Pure cotton is a poor conductor of heat and provides much better insulation than other types of fabric/wadding. Polyester wadding is a good conductor of heat, and using it for oven gloves will probably result in a lot of dropped dishes.

Hand-Dyed Fabrics

A range of hand-dyed cotton fabrics are available from www.time4me-workshops.co.uk/shop.

Machine Setup

All seam allowances are ¼" (1 cm) unless stated otherwise.

A 2.5 mm stitch length is used throughout except for the addition of appliqué images.

A standard zigzag foot is used throughout.

To Make Your Oven Glove
Cut Out Your Oven Glove Pieces
   Technique: Accurate Measuring >
   From the main color, measure and cut out:
   1 x rectangle 19" x 6" (48 cm x 15 cm)
   2 x squares 6" (15 cm)
   2 x squares 8-¼" (21 cm)

   Technique: Rotary Cutting >
   From the contrast color, measure and cut out:
   2 x strips 1-¾" x 19" (4.5 cm x 48 cm)
   4 x strips 6" x 1-¾" (15 cm x 4.5 cm)
   4 x 8-¼" x 1-¾" strips (21 cm x 4.5 cm)
   2 x squares 8-¼" (21 cm)
   2 x rectangles 19" x 8-¼" (48 cm x 21 cm)
   1 x rectangle for the hanging loop 7" x 1-½" (17.5 cm x 4 cm)

Assemble Oven Glove Main Panel
With right sides together, stitch the 19" x 1-¾" contrast strips to the long edges of the 19" x 6" rectangle.

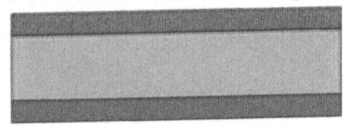

   Press the seam allowances open.
   Technique: Pressing for a Professional Finish >

Place the 8-¼" main color squares one on each end of the rectangle, wrong sides together. Line up one of the sides of each square with the short ends of the rectangle. Pin these ends together.

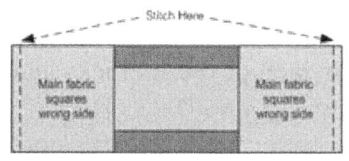

Stitch the 8-¼" main color squares to the short ends of the rectangle.

Open out the squares and press seam allowances towards the squares.

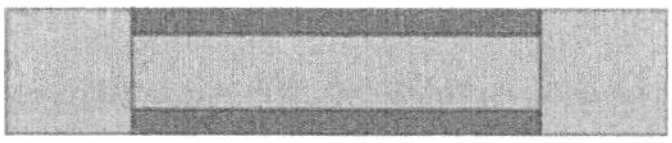

Make the Hand Pockets

Take one of the 6" main color squares and stitch two of the 6" contrast strips to opposite sides. Press seam allowances open.

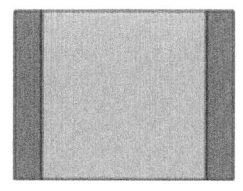

Stitch two of the 8-¼" strips to the remaining sides. Press seam allowances open.

Repeat with the remaining 6" main color square.

Using a dry iron, set to the wool setting, fuse an 8-¼" square of interfacing to the rear of each of these blocks.

Tip: Choosing and Using Interfacing >

Now place one of the 8-¼" contrast squares right sides together on top of each of these blocks and stitch down one edge, creating a ¼" seam.

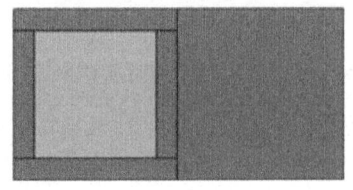

Open out blocks and press seam towards the edged block. Fold the plain square over onto the rear of the edged square and press with wrong sides together to form a faced block.

Add Your Heart Appliqués

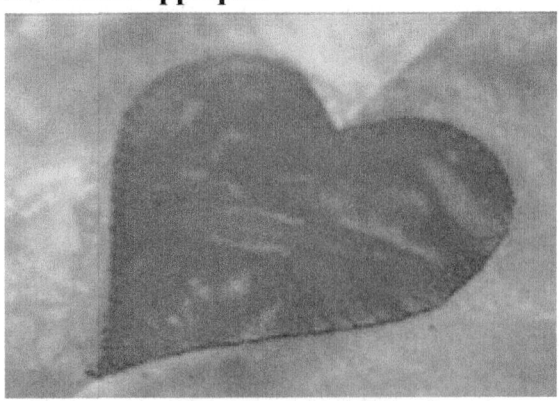

If you want to add an appliqué design, then you can do this now.

Technique: Creating Appliqué Designs >

Trace the heart image, below, onto the fusible web five times, keeping the images close together.

Roughly cut out the block of hearts. If you are using fusible web, which has two paper backings, remove one paper backing, ensuring that the glue layer remains with the side on which you have traced your image.

Position the block of hearts onto the wrong side of a piece of the contrast fabric. When you are happy with the positioning, press in place using a dry iron set to the wool setting. Allow to cool.

Note:

If you only have one iron and don't want to risk getting glue on the soleplate, you can increase the iron temperature a little and use a pressing cloth when fusing your appliqué images.

Carefully cut out each heart.

Remove the paper backing from two of the hearts, and place in the center of each of the hand pocket blocks, orientating the hearts as required. In the following diagram, the seam joining the facing and the block is at the bottom.

Fuse in place.

Set your sewing machine for a narrow zigzag or blanket stitch and stitch around the heart shapes, through the pocket top and facing.

Fuse and stitch the remaining three hearts to the main section of the glove as shown.

Assemble Your Oven Glove

Lay the main section of the glove on a flat surface, right side up.

Place the hand pockets on each end, right side up with the seam facing towards the center of the glove and the raw outer edges aligned.

Stitch together the two 19" x 8-¼" rectangles along one of their short edges. Press seam open.

Place this piece on top of the glove panel followed by the two pieces of batting.

Tip: Selecting and Using Wadding >

Trim all the layers to the same size.

Ensuring that the hand pockets remain in position, pin layers together all the way round, leaving a 6" gap along one of the long edges for turning.

Stitch ½" in from the edge, beginning at one side of the gap and finishing at the other side.

Using scissors, trim the batting close to the seams.

Turn right side out and press.

Make a Hanging Loop

Take the fabric cut for the hanging loop and iron over ¼" on one long edge.

Turn in the other long edge to the center of the fabric and iron.

Fold the first edge into the center covering the raw edge.

Pin and stitch one line of stitching along the length of the piece.

Note:

Placing the pins at right angles rather than in-line with the edge means you can leave them in place while sewing.

Position the hanging loop in the center of the glove and stitch to the seam allowance of the gap left open for turning.

Close the gap with neat hand-stitching.

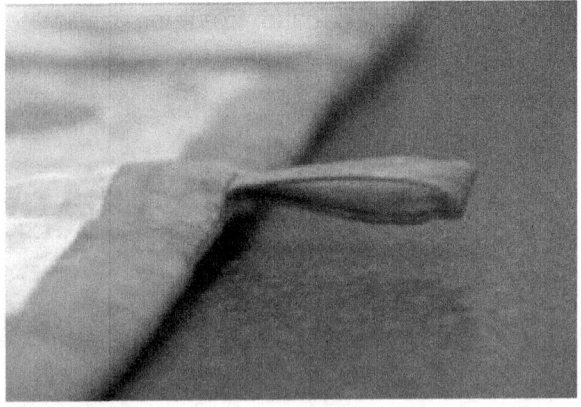

Technique: Basic Hand Sewing >
…and you're done!

Tablecloth

This fun tablecloth will draw admiring comments at your summer barbecue, but the border and colors could also be customized for other seasons, such as using leaves for autumn and Christmas images for the festive season. In this project you will learn how to create one of the most common patchwork design patterns, called "flying geese," and how to do free-machine embroidery.

You Will Need:

3 toning fat quarters in each of four colors. I used three different values (light, medium and dark) in violet, cherry, green and orange.

- 1 m fabric for wide borders
- 1-½ m fabric for backing. If your fabric is only 45" wide, you will need to join it to make the 47" width.

- ½ m fabric for binding
- Fabric scraps for appliqué images
- 1 m Steam-a-Seam for appliqué images
- Template for appliqué images

Hand-Dyed Fabrics

A range of hand-dyed cotton fabrics are available from www.time4me-workshops.co.uk/shop.

Machine Setup

All seam allowances are ¼" (1 cm) unless stated otherwise.

A 2.5 mm stitch length is used throughout except for the addition of appliqué images.

A standard zigzag foot is used throughout except for the addition of appliqué images.

To Make Your Tablecloth

Cut Out Your Fabric

Cut out the following pieces:
- 5 x squares 5-¼" (13 cm) in the light or medium value of each of the four colors
- 20 x squares 27/8" (7.5 cm) in the light or medium value of each of the four colors
- 10 x squares 2-½" x 8-½" (6-½ cm x 21-½ cm) in the dark value of each of the four colors
- 4 x strips 32" x 8-½" (81-½ cm x 21-½ cm) for wide borders
- 1 x backing piece 47" x 47" (120 cm x 120 cm) Technique: Rotary Cutting >

Make Your Flying Geese Squares

Lay one 5-¼" square face up on a flat surface.

Place two 27/8" squares (in the same color range) face down on the larger square.

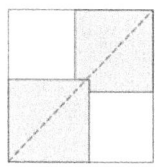

Draw a diagonal line through both small squares as shown.

Check that your needle is in the center position and line up one edge of your presser foot with the diagonal line. Stitch. Repeat on the other side of the line.

Technique: Finishing Edges >

Using a rotary cutter and ruler, cut along the diagonal line.

Press the small triangles away from the large ones, pressing the seam allowance towards the large triangle.

Technique: Pressing for a Professional Finish >

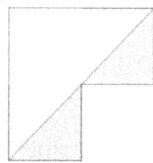

Place one small square face down on each of the two triangle pieces and draw a diagonal line as shown.

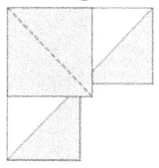

Stitch, as before, on either side of the diagonal line.

Cut along the diagonal line.

Press the small triangles away from the large one, pressing the seam allowances towards the large triangle. This makes one flying geese panel. Make a further three in the same way.

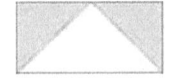

Join the four panels to form a block as shown below.

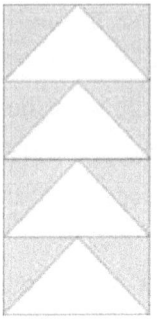

Lay one of the 2-½" x 8-½" strips (in the same color range), wrong side up along one of the long edges of the block. Pin in place. Repeat with another strip on the other long edge of the block.

Stitch the strips onto the blocks. Press seams towards long strips.

Make all 20 blocks in the same manner.

Press thoroughly.

Using a quilter's square and rotary cutter, trim all blocks to 8-¼" squares.

Assemble Your Tablecloth Center

Arrange 16 of the blocks into a pleasing arrangement. An example is shown below. See the photograph for some color arrangement ideas.

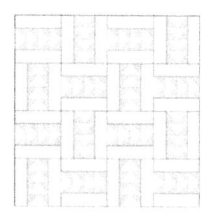

Lay the first block face down onto the second and pin the edge to be stitched. Stitch. Join the remaining blocks in the row. Seam allowances will naturally lie in the direction they need to be pressed.

Complete remaining rows in a similar manner.

Lay row 1 face down onto row 2 and pin in place, lining up seams accurately. Stitch, making sure that all seam allowances stay lying in the direction they were pressed.

Repeat with remaining rows.

Give the whole piece a good steam press, ensuring seam allowances stay in position.

Make Your Borders

Trace the appliqué shapes onto fusible web. Group similar items together as closely as possible. To create the design shown at the beginning of this project, you will need:
- 4 x orange outlines
- 32 x orange segments
- 4 x apple outlines
- 4 x apple cores

- 4 x bunches of grapes
- 4 x grape stalks
- 24 x cherries (or more, if you particularly like cherries)

Using scissors, roughly cut out each group of shapes, keeping those of the same color together.

Remove one paper backing from the pieces, ensuring that the glue layer remains with the remaining paper backing (the one you traced the shapes onto).

Finger press each group of shapes onto the appropriate color fabric.

Press with a medium dry iron.

Carefully cut out the shapes and divide them into four groups, with sufficient pieces for each border in each group. Press one of the border pieces and lay it flat on the table.

Arrange the appliqué shapes until you are happy with the design. An example is shown below for the main fruits. Add as many cherries as you like!

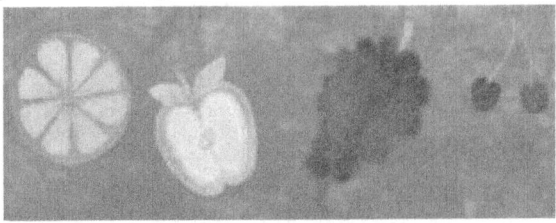

Once you are satisfied with the design, remove the paper backings and press the pieces into place using a medium iron.

Set your machine for free-machine embroidery and, using appropriately colored machine-embroidery threads, stitch pieces in place. Add lines for the orange segments and circles for grapes.

Technique: Free-machine Embroidery >

Note:
If you have not had a lot of experience in free-machine embroidery, you may prefer to secure your appliqué shapes with a narrow zigzag or blanket stitch.

Add embroidered (or satin-stitch) cherry stalks.

Repeat for remaining border pieces.

Assemble Your Tablecloth
Lay one of the border pieces face down along one edge of your flying geese panel, lining up the raw edges. Pin in place. Repeat with another border piece on the opposite edge. Stitch in place.

Open out the borders and press the seam allowances toward the borders.

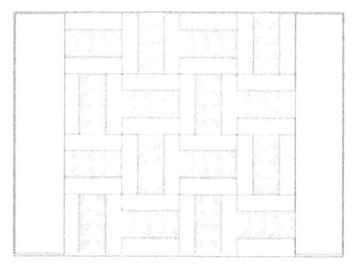

Take one of the remaining 8-½" border pieces and attach one flying geese block to each end, ensuring that the seams line up with the joining seam lines of the first two borders.

Stitch the borders, with the flying geese panels attached, to the tablecloth as shown below.

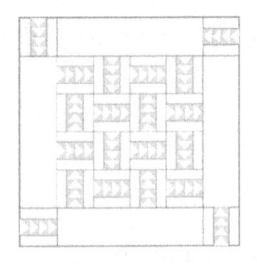

Press all border seam allowances towards borders.

Give the backing fabric a good press and lay it flat on the table.

Lay the tablecloth on top and carefully cut backing to the same size.

Securely pin together the tablecloth top and backing.

Using a walking foot if you have one, quilt (using a 3 mm stitch) along all of the seam lines, which join the flying geese panels together, ensuring the backing remains flat.

Technique: Basic Machine Quilting >

Add Your Binding

Prepare a double-thickness binding strip(s) and iron down the center.

Technique: Binding Edges >

Pin your binding to your tablecloth.

Machine-stitch the binding in place on one side, then fold the binding over the edge of the tablecloth and hand-stitch the other side using a neat slip stitch.

Remove pins from the binding.

Give the whole tablecloth a final good steam press and admire!

Technique: Pressing for a Professional Finish >

SEWING EVEN A MONKEY CAN DO

…and you're done!

Fabric Storage Box

This box is incredibly easy to make and can be made in any size. All you need is the willingness to be creative and a weakness for storage boxes. Don't limit yourself to just cotton, and don't hesitate to use different fabrics such as old denim jeans or silky polyester.

You Will Need:
    2 x squares of fabric
    1 x square of interfacing
    Tailor's chalk
    Ruler
    What you will learn:
    Fusing interfacing

Cut the Fabric to Size

Cut out two equal squares of fabric. You can even use fabric scraps, sew them together and trim to a square. The fabric below measures 12" x 12".

Fuse the Interfacing

Take one square and place the interfacing on top, with the shiny part facing the fabric. For best results, read the instructions of your interfacing. Some interfacings require a higher fusing temperature than others.

Once you have fused the pieces together, trim off any excess interfacing.

Sew the Pieces Together

Place the squares on top of each other, right sides facing. Sew together with a ¼" seam allowance. Leave an opening on one side, so you can turn the piece inside out later on. Use a backstitch on each end of the stitch so the seam doesn't open up as you work with the piece.

Turn the Piece Inside Out

Snip off a tiny piece at each corner, making sure not to cut off the actual stitch. Then grab the corners and pull them through the opening.

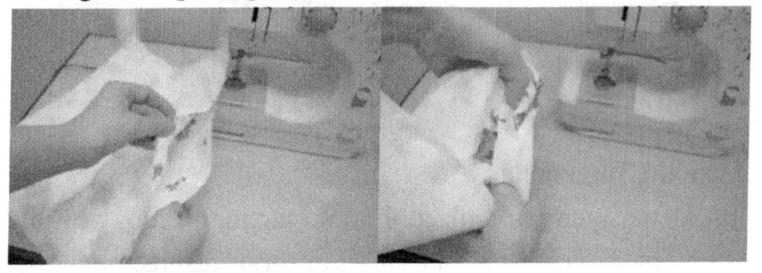

Sew the opening shut with a top stitch.

Marking

Iron the piece if needed, then fold it in half. Measure the short side and make a marking at the center. Then mark the same distance on the long-folded edge.

For example, if your short edge is 6", then you make a marking at 3". Moving on to the long-folded edge, mark 3" from the outer corner. Unite the two points with tailor's chalk.

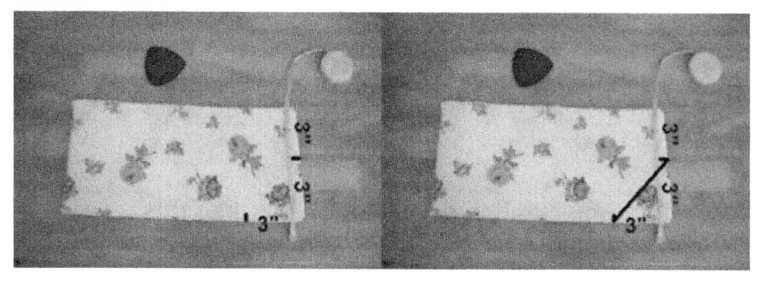

Sew the Wedges

Sew a straight stitch on the marked line.

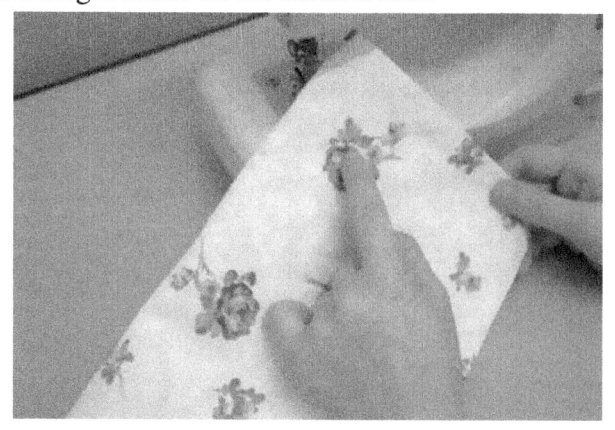

Once done, place the right edge on the adjacent and sew another straight stitch.

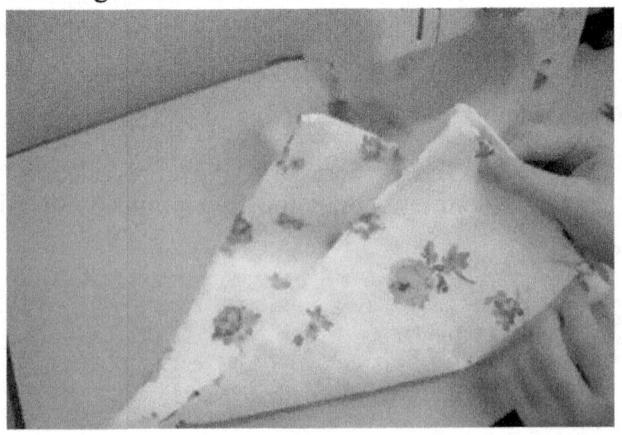

After doing so, the piece should look like this:

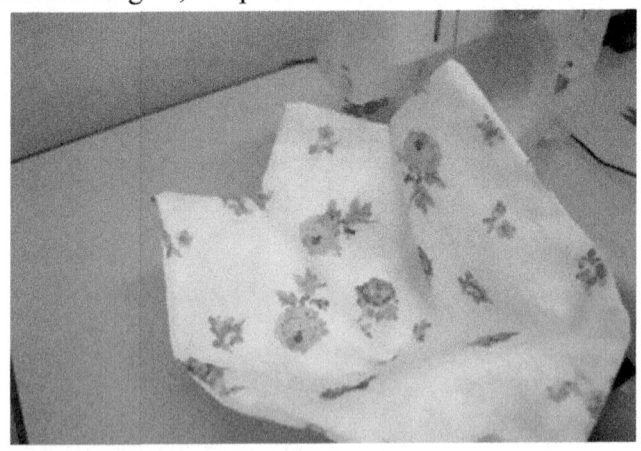

Repeat this method with the remaining two edges.

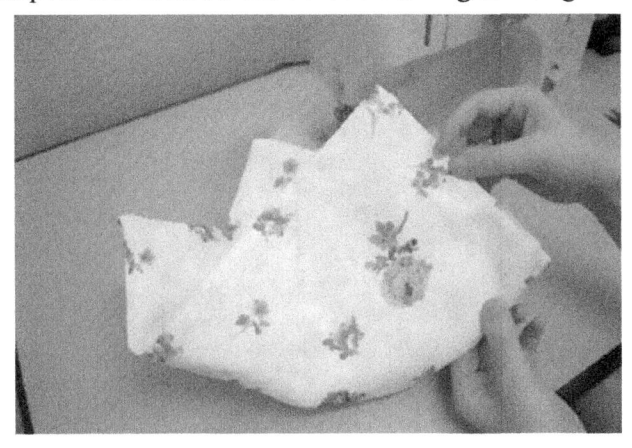

Once finished, your piece should look like this:

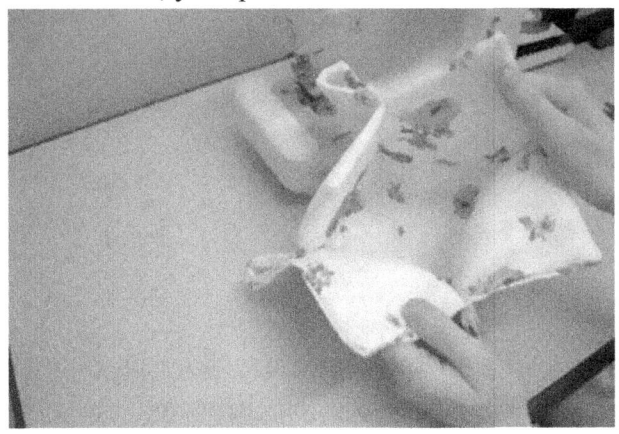

Finishing Touches

Turn the piece inside out. You can leave the box as it is, or you can hand-stitch the four flaps into place, using a button on each outer corner.

Multi-Purpose Tool Organizer

This project has a lot in common with the previous storage box, only it stores your precious items in a different way. The following technique serves as a guideline. For this project, I used a makeup brush set as an example. The fabric is a thick yet soft satin that will give the toolkit an elegant look. By varying fabrics and size, you can adapt this project to your needs. For example, rough, thick cotton, old denim jeans or upholstery scraps will create a toolkit for heavier tools such as hammers or screwdrivers. Just follow your creative instinct!

You Will Need:
- 3 x fabric rectangles
- 1 x fusible interfacing
- Tailor's chalk
- Measurement tape
- What you will learn:
- Attaching ribbon
- Topstitching compartments

Cutting

Determine the size of your project by using an item as a guideline. The item should be placed such that it has enough space around it. Cut out the lining, the interfacing and the main fabric to the same size.

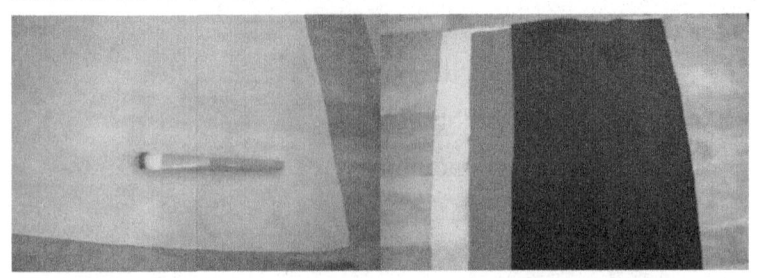

Fusing

Fuse the interfacing to either the lining or the main fabric. Since the main fabric was already thick enough, I decided to enforce the lining instead.

Cut and Sew the Pocket

With your item, make a rough measurement for the pocket. Note that it should be twice the size so it can be folded in half. This will later create a crisp and clean edge.

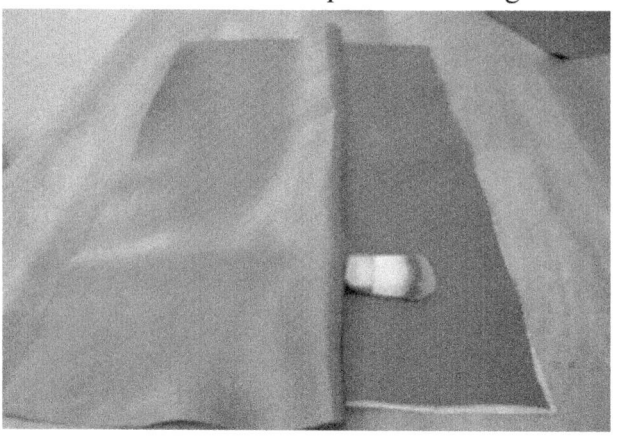

Once you have determined the size of the pocket, line up the fabric inside out and stitch with a ¼" seam allowance. Then turn the pocket inside out and press with the seam running through the middle of the piece. This will ensure nice and even compartments.

Place the pressed pocket onto the lining fabric and pin. You want to pin the piece with the inner seam running down. Sew the two pieces together to create one wide pocket. Make a backstitch at each end to secure.

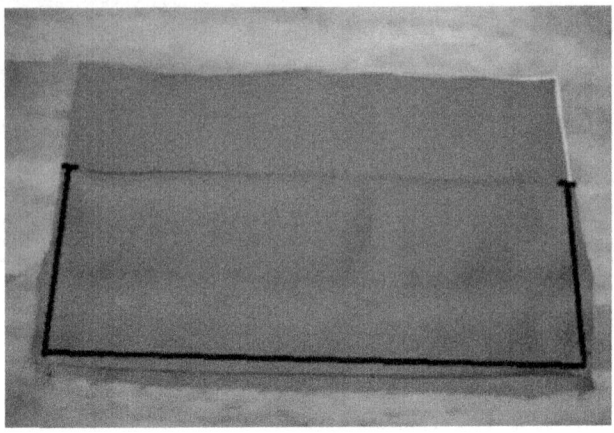

Here you can see the seam facing down:

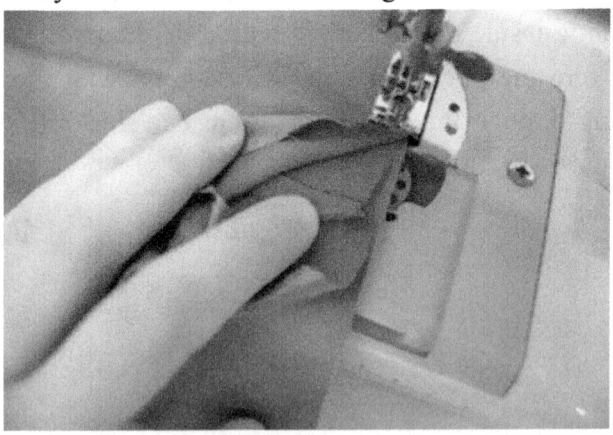

Sew the Compartments

It is time to take out all your tools and place them on the project. This way you can decide how wide or narrow you need your compartments to be. In the case of the makeup brushes, the compartments are of similar width. In other cases, the compartments can vary from narrow to wide.

Mark the compartments with tailor's chalk and a ruler, then top stitch. To prevent the seams from opening up later on, backstitch every time you reach the upper edge.

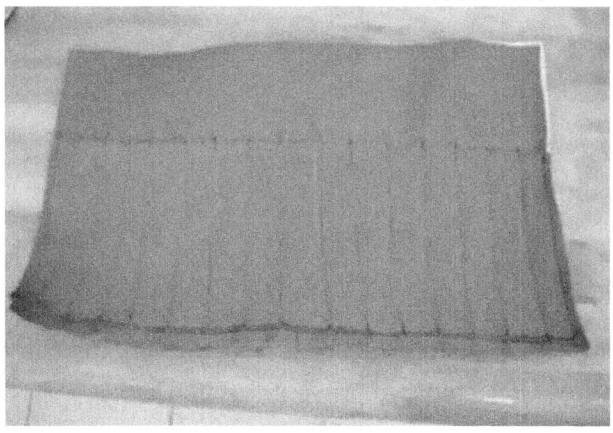

Stitch the Main Fabric

Place the main fabric onto the compartments, right sides facing, and pin together.

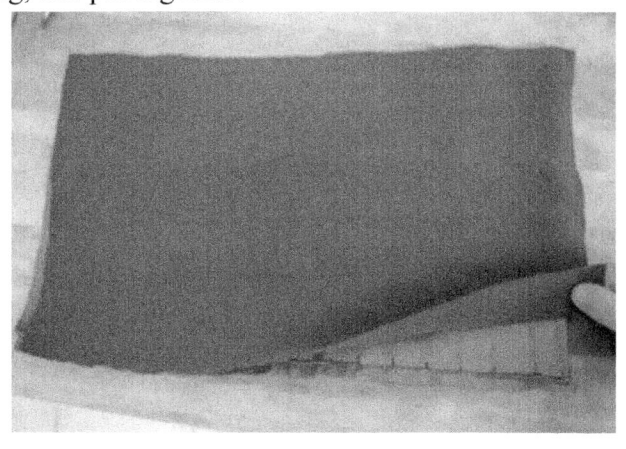

Take a matching ribbon and cut a strip that is twice the width of your project. You will be able to trim off the excess later.

If you are working with a synthetic ribbon, carefully burn the ends with a candle to prevent fraying.

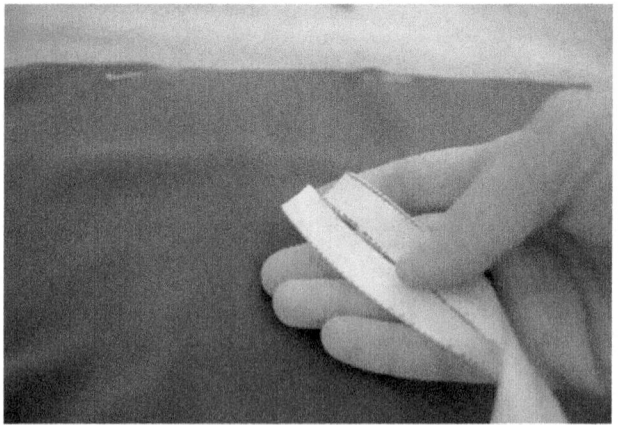

Fold the ribbon in half and make a loose knot. Then slide the ribbon in between the fabrics, with a little fold sticking out.

SEWING EVEN A MONKEY CAN DO

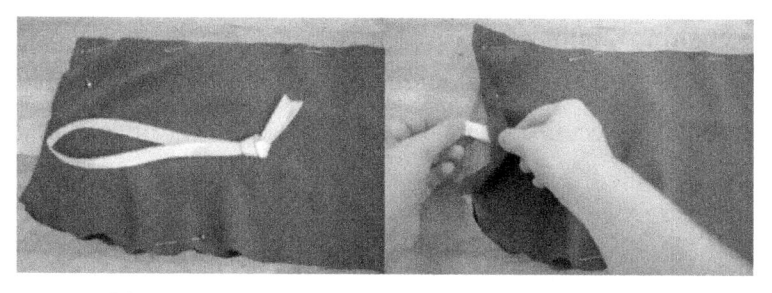

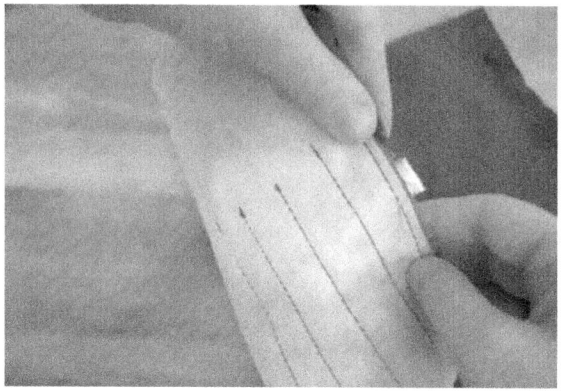

Sew the pieces together, leaving an opening at the bottom. Through this opening, you will be able to turn the project inside out.

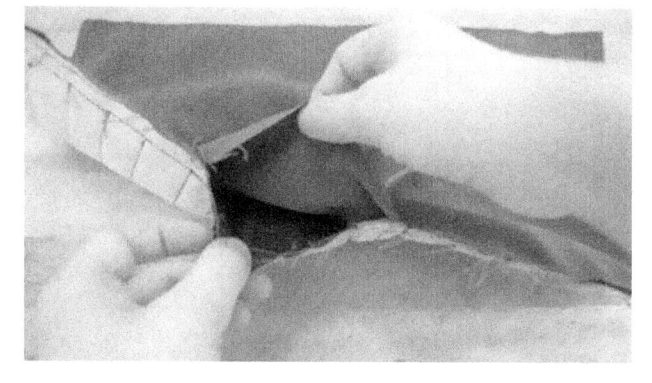

Finishing Touches

Snip off the corners without cutting through the seam. Then turn the project inside out and press. Close the bottom opening with a seam.

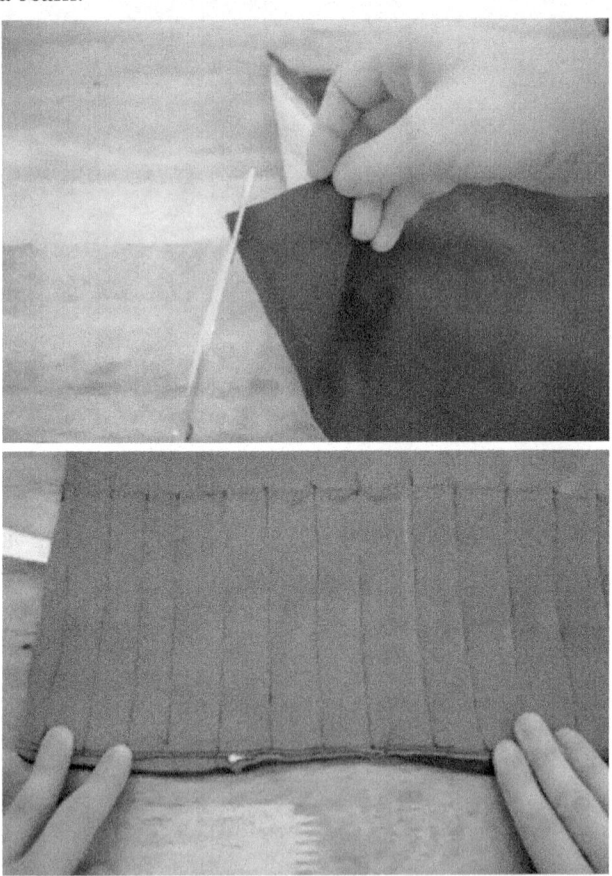

Plain Shirt

You Will Need:
   Wrist
   Neck
   Buttonholes and buttons
   Wrist fitting

You will find a tutorial for mounting the wrist on the Poitiers Academy website. I still give you four of my little tips that will be useful if, like me, you make the choice to make your wrist with two pieces:

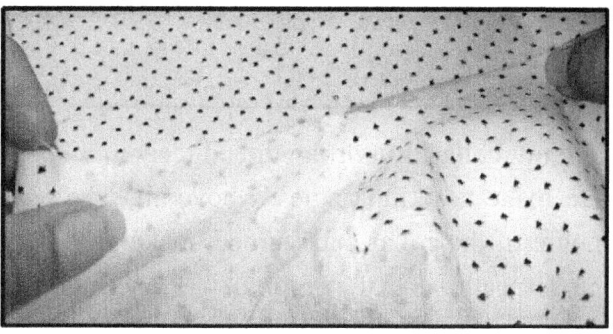

For the fusible, I advise you to hollow out the corners before applying it. Forming the wedge will be easier and you will have less thickness when you topstitch.

When you join the two sides of the wrist, you can slip in a piece of wire to help you form the corner. When you reach the end of your side, slide the thread and make a stitch by turning the hand wheel to wedge the thread in the seam. Turn your fabric to sew the other side, lift the presser foot and slide the thread between the two fabrics, then continue your sewing. When turning your wrist to form the corners, you just have to pull on the thread – after, obviously, having hollowed out the corners and opened the seams.

When overstitching the wrists, you can slip a thread in the two corners to help your machine pass this thickness by pulling (gently) on the thread

Collar

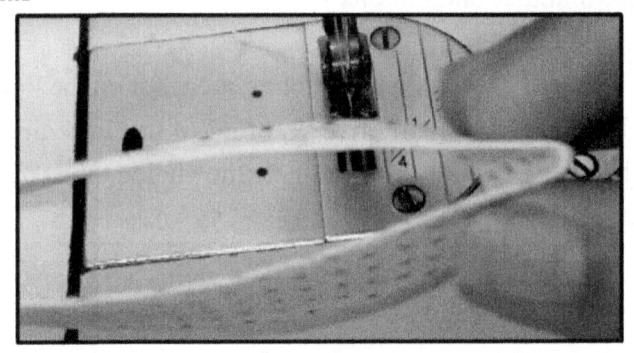

To make my collar, I used the thread technique mentioned above to make beautiful angles. Above all, when you iron the amount of the collar once turned, make sure to roll the seam underneath so that it is invisible once the collar is fitted.

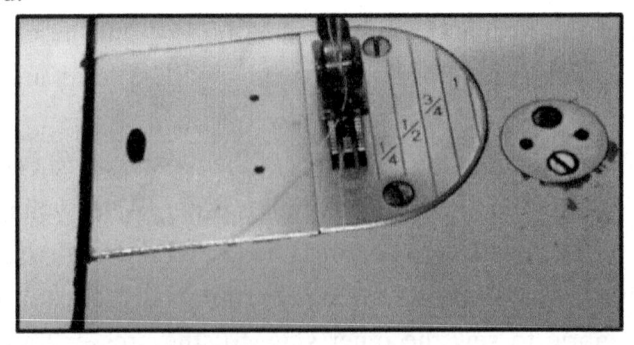

Buttonholes and Buttons
Making the buttonholes is a delicate step. First of all, care must be taken to put them on the right side. For women, the buttonholes are on the right and the buttons on the left.

To place the buttons, here are the rules to follow:
Place a button on the chest line
Place a button on the waistline
Place the first button 5 or 6 cm from the neck

I advise you to take your time and give it a try. Making the buttonholes is a delicate step. It is the execution of the finishing touches that makes the quality of the garment. Once the location of the buttonholes is chosen, I advise you to do several tests for the size of the buttonholes with the buttons you have chosen.

Sewing a shirt is good training for CAP. This allows you to perform some techniques that you must master for the exam.

Basic Pajama Pants

If you are starting out in the world of sewing, don't worry; making your own pants is not excessively complicated. Of course, before starting it is best that you inform yourself about the steps you must follow.

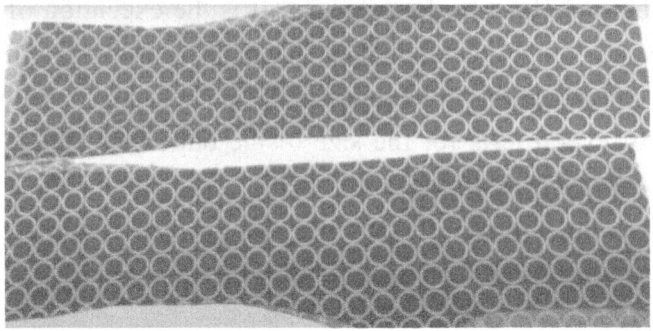

Choose the Fabric

In order for you to be able to move once you have them on, the fabric of the pants should be light, pleasant and solid. If you are just starting, we advise you to use a cotton fabric, which will be easy to sew and manipulate.

Avoid fabrics that are difficult to work with, such as knitting, which is stretchy, or silk, which slips. Adapt the choice of fabric to the type of pants you want (satin, taffeta, to wear; denim, linen, etc., for a more informal look).

Choose a Pant Pattern

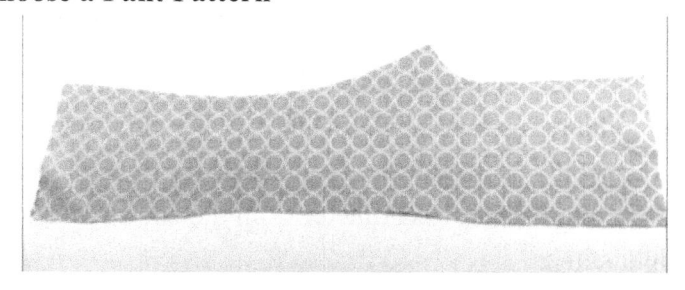

We recommend that you look for a pattern to make your own pants. The best thing is to choose one that has already been tried, or that you start by making a test pair of pants with a fabric that does not cost much. The simplest pants are those with an elastic waist.

For the rest, the pattern should be more precise. The same goes for the U-shaped seam used between the legs – the pattern should serve as an accurate guide, without risking disappointing results.

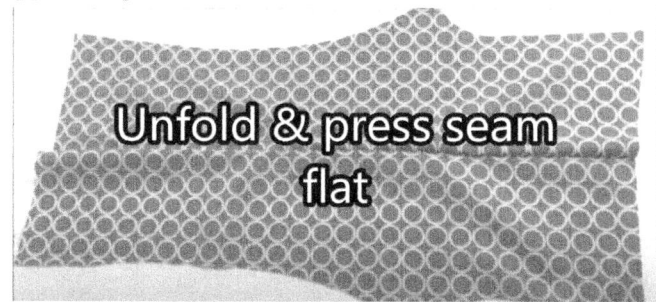

Put the Pant Legs Together

Depending on the pattern you choose, you must put together the different pieces that make up the pants legs in one way or another. You must puncture the pieces and join the pieces of fabric that make up the front part of the leg and then the back part.

If your pants have pockets, remember to sew them before joining the legs. Once sewn together, place the front of one leg against the back and start to puncture the outer sides and then the inner sides, 1 centimeter from the edge and using a straight stitch.

Sew the Union of the Legs

The union of the legs is one of the most delicate parts in the manufacturing of pants, but with a good pattern and a little patience, you will achieve it without any problem. Lay the two legs side by side, crotch to crotch joint and waist to waist. Next, use pins to mark the seam and stitch a centimeter from the edge, with a straight stitch.

Final Touch

Once you have successfully completed these big steps, all you have to do is finish the pants: waist, hem, buttons, zipper or buttons for the fly… You decide the final touch!

Hot Water Bottle Cover

Make this as a gift for someone special or just treat yourself. The large top flap on the top of this cover allows for easy filling of the bottle and a hanging loop allows for easy storage. The images given are just a suggestion; any winter or sleep related motif would be suitable. In this project you will learn how to make a split back (to insert the hot water bottle) and gain more practice in quilting.

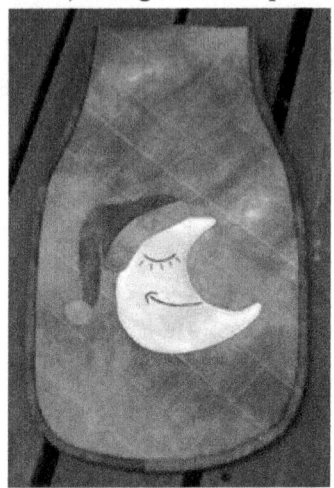

This project makes a single hot water bottle cover for any size of hot water bottle.

You Will Need:
- ½ m of sturdy cotton fabric
- 1 x fat quarter of contrast cotton fabric for piping
- ½ m of pure cotton batting
- ½ m thin cotton for lining
- ½ m fusible web
- Scraps of fabric for appliqué

- 1" square of Velcro for flap
- Toning threads
- Hot water bottle

Hand-Dyed Fabrics

A range of hand-dyed cotton fabrics are available from www.time4me-workshops.co.uk/shop.

Machine Setup

All seam allowances are ¼" (1 cm) unless stated otherwise.

A 2.5 mm stitch length is used throughout except for the addition of appliqué images.

A standard zigzag foot is used throughout.

Fabric Cutting

For accuracy, all cutting should be done using a quilter's ruler and/or square and rotary cutter, unless stated otherwise. The exception to this is when cutting out appliqué images, for which scissors can be used.

To Make Your Hot Water Bottle Cover
Cut Out Your Pattern

Lay a large sheet of paper (any sort will do) out on a flat surface and place your (empty) hot water bottle on it.

Draw round the bottle, adding a ½" seam allowance all the way round.

Cut one back piece the size of the template.

Using the template as a pattern, cut out one front piece, extending the top so it is long enough to fold over the top of the bottle and fasten on the other side.

Using the front and back pieces as patterns, cut out one of each of batting and lining.

Tip: Selecting and Using Wadding >

Add Your Appliqué

If you want to add an appliqué design, then you can do this now.

Technique: Creating Appliqué Designs >

Trace the appliqué image onto fusible web.

Roughly cut around each shape and, using a dry iron set to the wool setting, press onto the back of the fabric you are using for the appliqué.

Carefully cut out the images from the fabric.

Arrange the images on the front outer panel of the cover and, once you are happy with the arrangement, press in place.

Set your sewing machine for a 3 mm wide, 2 mm long zigzag stitch and, using a toning thread, carefully stitch around the images.

Note:
If you prefer to use blanket stitch instead of zigzag, this would be equally effective. If you do decide to use free-machine embroidery, place the lining and batting panel behind the front outer panel before you stitch the image pieces in place, stitching through all three layers.

Quilt Your Cover

Technique: Basic Machine Quilting >

Take the lining panel for the front cover and lay out on a flat surface. Lay the front batting panel on top followed by the front cotton panel, right side up.

Note:

There are a number of ways in which this project can be quilted, depending on your personal taste. You could either quilt around the image, or if you are experienced in free-machine quilting, you could make an all-over star pattern. Personally, I prefer to crosshatch quilt a project such as this.

Pin the three layers together securely.

Fit a walking foot – if you have one – to your sewing machine and, using toning thread and a 3 mm straight stitch, quilt the front panel, stopping at the edges of the image and continuing on the other side so the image remains unquilted. Ensure that you do a few reverse stitches when stopping and starting at the edges of the image, or the stitches may begin to unravel.

Note:

You are probably wondering if it wouldn't be easier to quilt the front panel before adding the image. I have tried this but find that the quilted lines show through the image when it is fused to the panel and detract from the effect.

Layer and quilt the back section with the crosshatch design.

Divide and Bind the Back Section

Take the back section and measure and mark a point 6" from the bottom of the panel. Cut the panel in half, widthways (from side to side) through this point.

Measure one of the edges you have just cut and cut two pieces of fabric of this length and 3" wide.

Technique: Finishing Edges >

Fold each piece in half lengthways and press.

Pin one piece to each of the cut edges, on the right side of the panel and with the raw edges together. Place your pins at 90 degrees to the edge so you can sew over them.

Note:

Sewing over pins is not as scary as it sounds, provided you slow down as you approach each pin. If the needle should hit a pin at a slow speed, it is likely to slide off, but if it hits at a high speed, it is likely to break the needle, or pin, or both.

Stitch both bindings in place.

Flip the binding over and press, then fold toward the back of the panel, lining the folded edge up with the line of stitching. Press and pin in place, again placing the pins at 90 degrees.

Repeat for the top edge of the back-top panel.

Stitch binding to both edges, from the right side of the panel, positioning your stitches 1/8" from the seam joining the binding to the panel.

Place the front panel face down on a table, then place the back panels on top, face up, lapping the top back binding over the lower back binding.

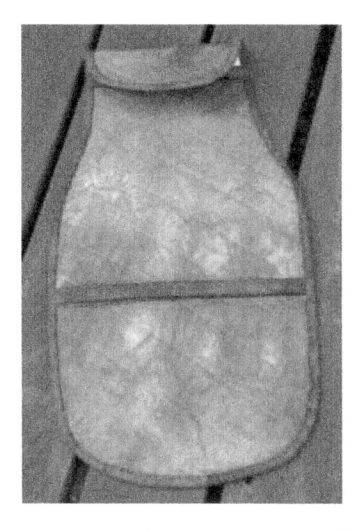

Pin the 6 layers together at several places around the panel.

Add Your Binding

Make the binding.

Technique: Binding Edges >

Turn the cover over so the front is facing upwards.

Starting at the center of the lower edge of the cover and leaving a 2" end, pin the binding all around the bottle cover front, raw edges together, finishing with a 2" end at the point where you started.

Note:
When pinning on the binding, ensure that you include the back panel and the wadding and lining of the extended top edge.

Open out the 2" ends, unpicking a few stitches if necessary, and pin them right sides together so they will lie flat against the edge of the cover.

Stitch and trim seam allowances to ½".

Press seam open.

Fold the binding in half to cover the seam, press and pin in place.

Make a Hanging Loop
- Cut a piece of leftover binding fabric about 6" long.
- Turn over one long edge ¼" and press.
- Turn over the other long edge ½" and press.
- Fold the first edge over the second, enclosing the raw edges, and press and pin at 90 degrees to the strip.
- Stitch down the center of the strip, close to the center fold.
- Fold strip in half and pin to the back lower edge, in the center, raw edges together, so the loop is pointing upwards.

- Stitch the binding all around the cover ¼" from the edge, securing the loop in place at the same time.
- Using scissors, trim around the edge of the cover so the edges are flush with the binding edges.
- Fold the binding over towards the back of the cover so the folded edge meets the stitching.
- Pin, press and stitch, using a neat slip stitch, in place.

Fasten Your Cover Top

Stitch one side (hook or loop) of your Velcro to the cover top back, ensuring it is centralized, and one to the underside of the flap.

…and you're done!

Table Runner

Make this simple table runner in a variety of colors to suit your mood. Then collect seasonal leaves and make appliqué shapes to decorate it. Choose the deciduous greens and yellows for summer, the bronze and red of fallen leaves for autumn, or holly and ivy for Christmas. For beginners, the runner can be left plain. In this project you will learn more about binding edges and gain confidence in using appliqué.

You Will Need:
3 x fat quarters in harmonizing shades (you won't need all this fabric but can use the leftovers to make the matching tablemats)

1 x fat quarter in a contrasting shade

½ m x 45" contrasting fabric for binding (use the remainder for the table mat binding)

¾ m pure cotton batting (at least 45" or 115 cm wide)

¾ m backing fabric (at least 45" or 115 cm wide). If you choose a decorative backing fabric, your table runner will be double-sided!

Toning polyester thread
Embroidery threads
1 m fusible web

Collect seasonal leaves from your garden or the park to make appliqué templates. Press flat between two sheets of kitchen paper and place between the pages of a heavy book. Alternatively, use the supplied templates.

What Is a "Fat Quarter"?
You may see "fat quarters" of fabric for sale in the shops. These are rough squares of fabric, generally for patchwork use, produced by cutting a meter (or a yard) length of a roll of fabric.

Rolls of fabric are typically 40 to 45 inches wide, depending on the manufacturer. The resultant strip of fabric (either 1 meter or 1 yard long by 40 to 45 inches wide) is then cut into four to create four fat quarters.

The minimum dimensions for a fat quarter should therefore be 18 x 20 inches, allowing you to get nine 6 x 6-inch squares for your patchwork. The edges are often not cut straight and will need "squaring up" with a rotary cutter and ruler.

Similarly, "fat eighths" are half this size (18 x 10 inches).

Hand-Dyed Fabrics
A range of hand-dyed cotton fabrics are available from www.time4me-workshops.co.uk/shop.

Machine Setup

All seam allowances are ¼" (1 cm) unless stated otherwise.

A 2.5 mm stitch length is used throughout except for the addition of appliqué images.

A standard zigzag foot is used throughout except for the addition of appliqué images.

Fabric Cutting

For accuracy, all cutting should be done using a quilter's ruler and rotary cutter, unless stated otherwise.

To Make Your Runner

From each of the three harmonizing fabrics, cut 5 pieces 3-½" x 11" (9 cm x 28 cm), giving 15 pieces in total.

Technique: Rotary Cutting >

From the contrasting fat quarter, cut 15 x 3-½" squares.

From the binding fabric, cut three strips 45" x 3" (115 cm x 8 cm).

From the batting, cut a piece 46" x 15" (117 cm x 38 cm).

From the backing fabric, cut a piece 46" x 15" (117 cm x 38 cm).

Make Your Runner Top

Place one of the contrasting squares, right sides together, against one of the short edges of one of the rectangles and stitch in place, leaving a ¼" seam.

Repeat for the remaining rectangles and squares.

Press the seam allowances towards the rectangles.

Technique: Pressing for a Professional Finish >

Arrange your blocks as shown in the diagram, moving the colors around until you are happy with the result.

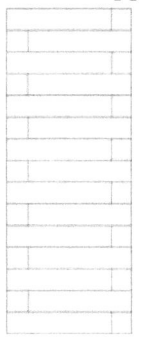

Starting at the top, place one of the blocks on top of the one immediately below, right sides together, and stitch along one of the long edges.

Repeat until all the blocks are joined together.

Press all the seam allowances open.

Quilt Your Runner

Place your backing fabric face down on a flat surface and lay the batting on top.

Lay the pieced and pressed runner on top, right side up.

Using long quilting pins (the flower-headed ones are good as they don't catch in the machine foot), place two pins along each of the long seams, at 90 degrees to the seam, through all three layers. Place the pins about 5" apart. Fit a walking foot to your machine if you have one.

Increase the machine stitch length to 3 mm.

Using a harmonizing thread on the top and a thread that matches the backing on the bobbin, quilt down each of the long seams, beginning near the center of the runner and working towards the ends.

Technique: Basic Machine Quilting >

Trim the runner so it measures 44" x 14" (112 cm x 36 cm).

Make Your Appliqué Leaves

If you want to add the appliqué leaves, then you can do this now. For alternative design ideas, see the following skill sheet.

Technique: Creating Appliqué Designs >

Trace the outlines of the leaves onto the fusible web and roughly cut out each leaf.

Press each leaf shape onto the back of the chosen fabric using a dry iron set to the wool setting.

Cut out leaf shapes carefully.

Remove the paper backing and position your leaves across the runner top.

When you are happy with their position, press in place.

Using free-machine embroidery, secure each leaf in place, adding veins and stalks as required.

Technique: Free-machine Embroidery >

Note:
If you don't feel confident enough to use free-machine embroidery, secure the leaves using a zigzag or blanket stitch.

Add Your Binding

Prepare a double-thickness binding strip(s) and iron down the center.

Technique: Binding Edges >

Pin your binding to your runner.

Machine-stitch the binding in place on one side, then fold the binding over the edge of the tablecloth and hand-stitch the other side using a neat slip stitch.

Remove pins from the binding.

Give the table runner a final good steam press and admire!

Technique: Pressing for a Professional Finish >

....and you're done!

JACOB JENSEN

Red Carpet Dress in 20 Minutes

Imperative: For this project, choose a heavy jersey that falls well and does not crumple. A little elastane is even better. The advantage, in addition to the wonderful fall, is that there is no need to hem!

Cut a square of 140 cm x 140 cm (applying yourself since the edges remain bare!). Allow more height if you are tall (I am 1.66 m!).

Fold the fabric in half crosswise and, 60 cm from the top, sew a 28 cm seam to join the two edges (the start should fall roughly at the level of your navel). The bottom remains open.

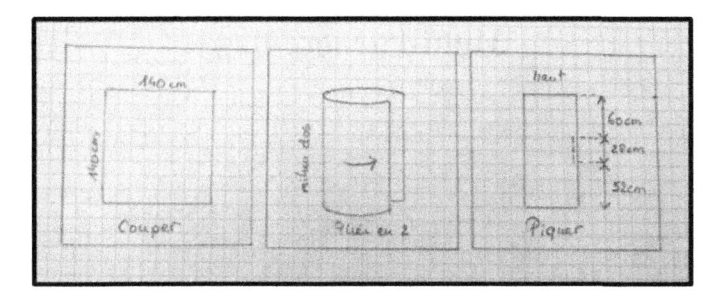

Turn right side out and put on the dress by positioning the seam in front, grabbing the two free sides from the top, pulling them to adjust the back, then crossing them twice just above the chest and tying them behind the neck like a pareo!

Adjust the hem if necessary.

Slip your new dress into your suitcase!

Here is a second idea – because I didn't stop there! Make a sarong dress to put on over your swimsuit. The cut is very simple, but the result is stunning; the drape forms all by itself at the neckline and lower back.

Multi-Purpose Bag

This project is slightly more complicated, but with the step-by-step picture guide you can create your own bag. As with most projects in this book, this bag can be done in any size, fabric and color combination.

For this project, you will need a fabric of your choice, lining fabric, interfacing and a zipper. The thicker the interfacing, the better. You can even use fusible batting instead for a sturdier result.

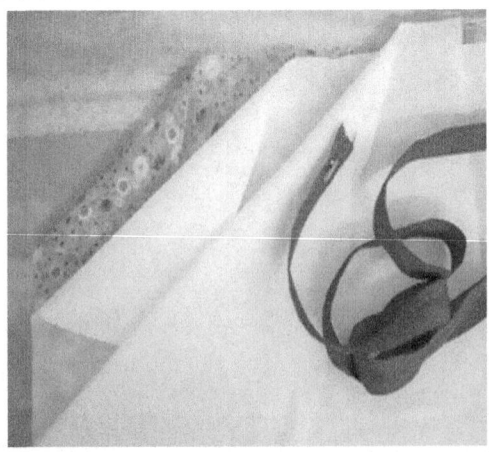

You Will Need:
- 2 x rectangles of fabric
- 1 x rectangle of interfacing or batting
- Tailor's chalk
- Measurement tape
- Ruler
- Zipper
- Zipper foot (optional)
- 6 strips of fabric for Hong Kong seam

What you will learn:
  Attaching a zipper
  Hong Kong seam

Cutting and Fusing

Although this bag can be done in any size, one rule is that you will need a rectangle shape. In the project below, the measurements are 20" x 15".

Cut the main fabric, the lining and the interfacing into equally large rectangles. Fuse the interfacing on the lining or the main fabric.

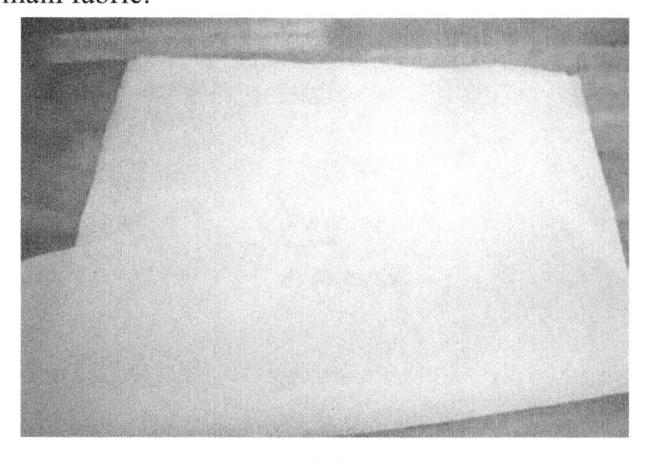

Attach the Zipper

Pin the zipper with its right side facing the right side of the main fabric. Then pin the lining onto the fabric, right sides facing. The zipper should be sandwiched between the two fabrics. Sew together with a straight stitch.

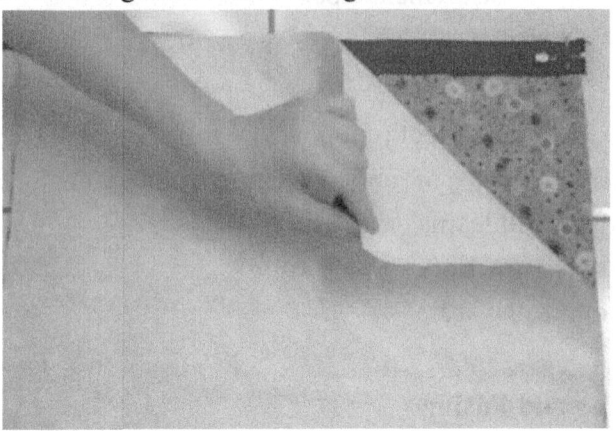

Using a Zipper Foot

A zipper foot gives a nicer and more professional look. It has two sides where it can be attached to the machine, making it easier to stitch as close to the zipper as possible. If you don't have a zipper foot, don't worry; just use a regular foot and set your machine to a left side stitch.

Sew the Zipper

Sew all three layers together – the lining, the zipper and the main fabric.

As you sew, you will notice that the slider will get in your way. Lift up the presser foot with the needle down, pull the slider a few inches down, then lower the foot and continue sewing.

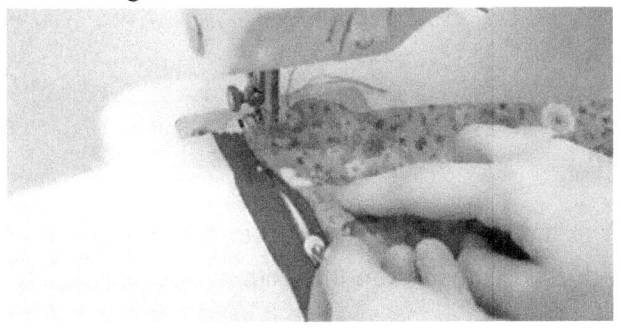

Once you catch up with the slider again, lift the presser foot and pull it back up.

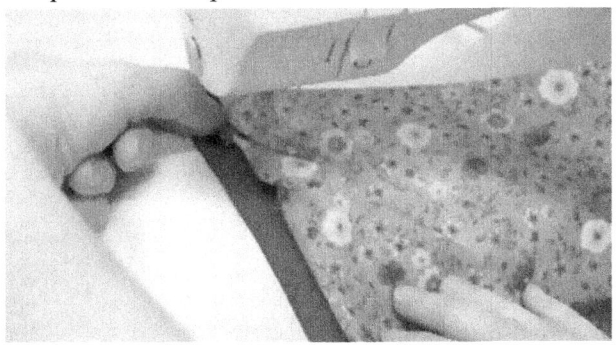

Pressing

Carefully iron along the zipper. Do not iron on top of the zipper if it's made of plastic.

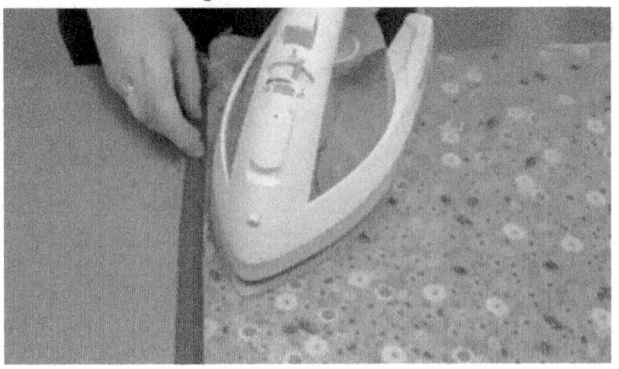

Trim the zipper if it's too long, then pin the end so the slider doesn't detach from the teeth by accident.

Attach the Other Side of the Zipper

Take the main fabric and pin it on the empty side of the zipper.

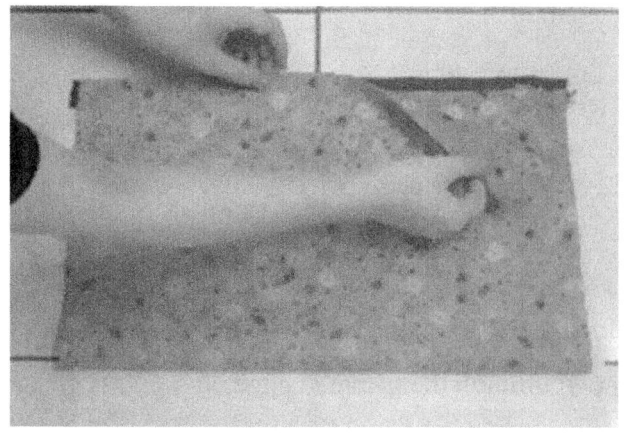

Fold the lining inwards. Again, the zipper will be sandwiched between the right sides of the fabrics. Sew the three pieces together.

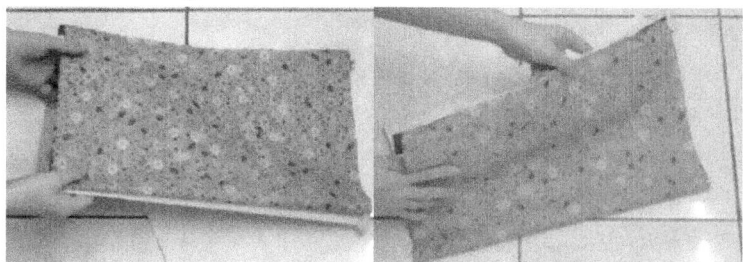

Open the Zipper

Once you have sewn both sides of the zipper, open up the piece. Notice that the wrong sides are facing out and the right sides are facing in.

Search for the zipper and open it up, being careful not to fully open through the trimmed edge.

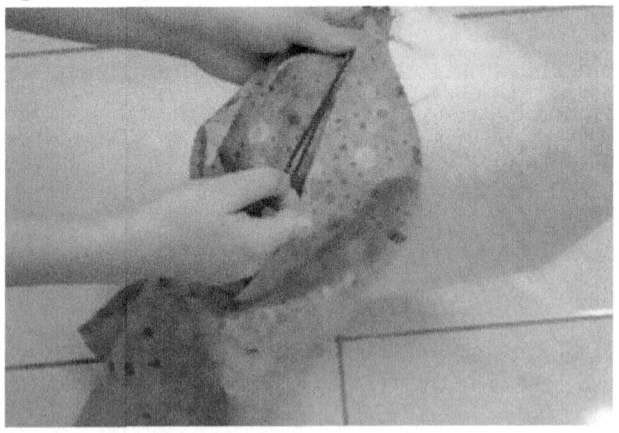

Pull out the lining through the opening.

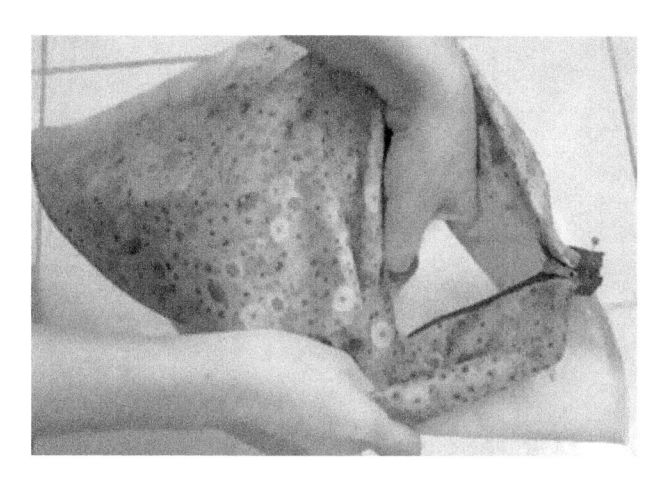

Trim and Sew the Edges

Lay out your piece with the zipper in the center. Trim off the frays if necessary.

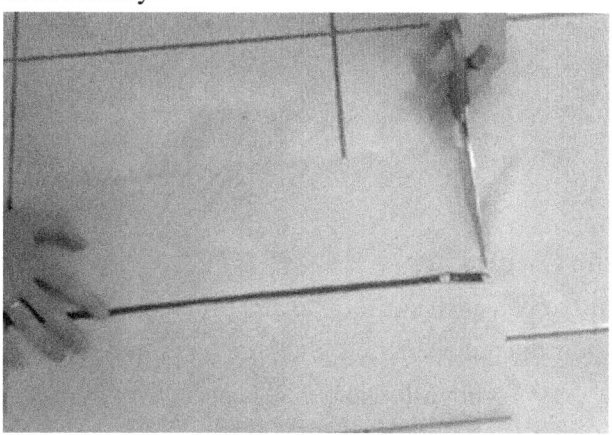

Sew the two raw edges on each side with a straight stitch and ¼" seam allowance.

Mark and Cut the Corners

On each corner, find the center between the outer edge and the zipper. Mark that distance on the long-folded edge too. Mark a small square on each corner, then cut out the corners.

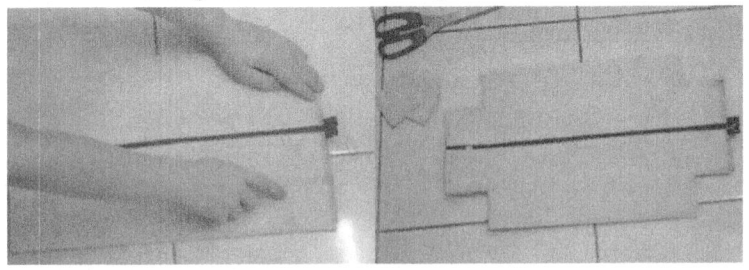

Sew the Corners

Carefully open each corner one at a time. Pull on the corners until their raw edges match. Seal the opening with a straight stitch of 1/8" seam allowance. Repeat on every corner.

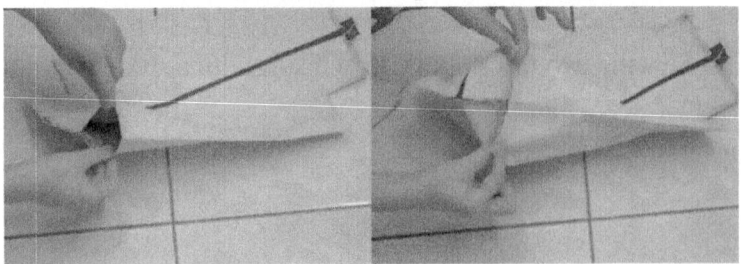

Seal with a Hong Kong Seam

Because you want your bag to be as sturdy as possible, a Hong Kong seam is a good choice for finishing the edges. For this, cut out 6 strips of fabric, each 1-¼" wide. The length depends on the bag. Two pieces should correspond to the horizontal edges (where the zipper starts and ends) and four strips will be used for each corner. Cut a bit longer than your measurement.

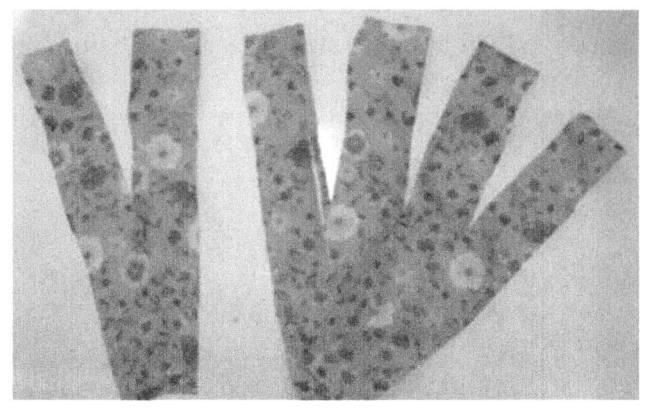

Start with the horizontal edges. Sew the strip on the bag, right sides facing. Pull the strip up, then turn the bag, fold the strip in half, and secure with pins if needed. Repeat on the other side.

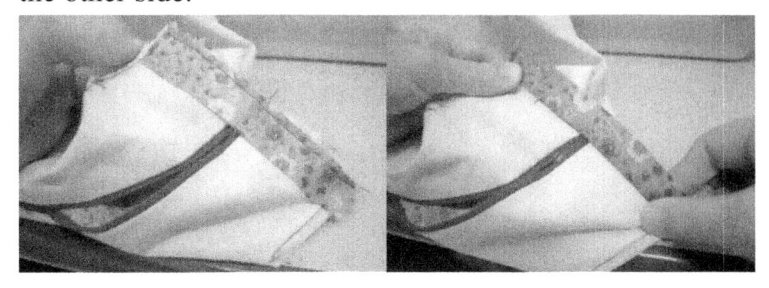

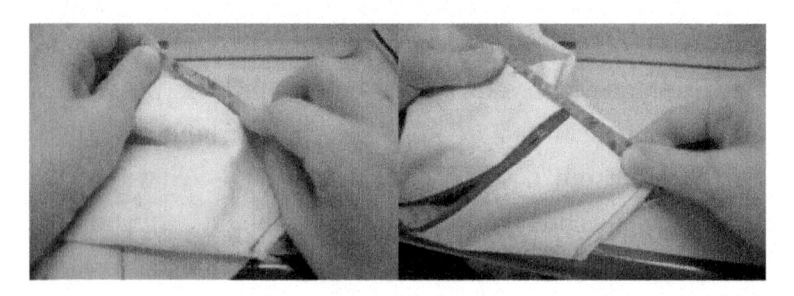

Moving on to the four remaining corner strips, repeat the process, but this time you need to create nice, clean ends. You can do so by folding the strip on each end before sewing it.

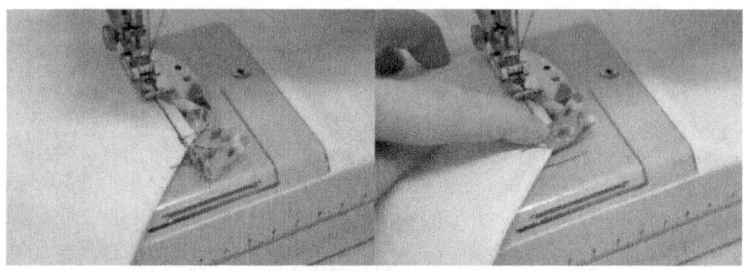

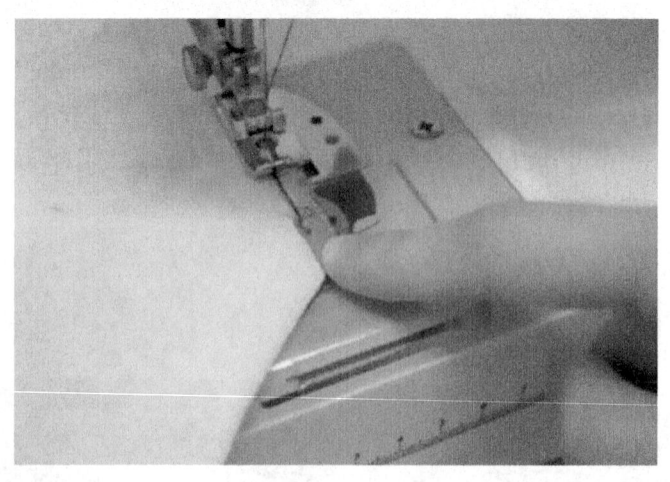

This is the end result:

Prepare the Straps

Turn the bag inside out. Decide what length you want your straps to be, then add another inch for the seam allowance.

For this model, you can use the two fabrics as shown below. The lining fabric is wider than the main fabric, so it creates nice, clean borders.

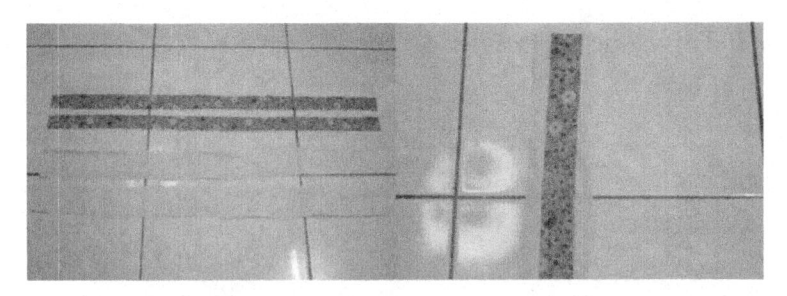

Double fold the bottom fabric on top of the main fabric. Then top stitch the straps.

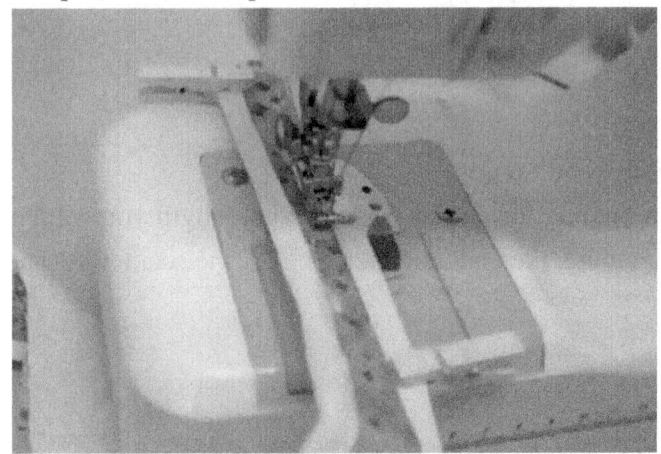

Attach the Straps

Stitch the straps on the bag, then lift up the straps and pin.

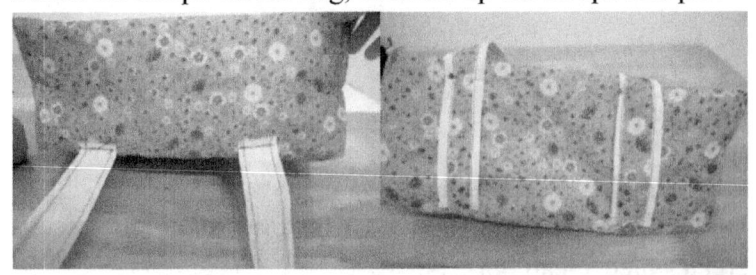

Topstitch the straps all the way to the upper edge of the bag.

Conclusion

I hope this book was able to help you to understand what sewing is about, learn about the materials you need, and learn how to make simple but high-quality projects that you will be proud of.

The next step is to make sure you have read this book carefully and that you're willing to put into practice what you have learned. Even if you make a mistake at first, what matters is that you tried – and are willing to try more! Remember that by keeping these guidelines in mind, you can learn to sew without wasting a lot of time, energy, or effort.

If you want to become a popping industrialist, pick the field of sewing. Believe me, you can get really famous in this area. Desires have changed. People prefer to find more and more chic and chill designs in their dresses.

I hope you now know some sewing basics. In order to become better at sewing, you will need to practice. Therefore, ensure you spend some time every week practicing until you perfect the art.

The do-it-yourself projects in this book are only some of the ideas you can use for your sewing room. You can always experiment or create storage boxes, shelves or organizers that suit your own sewing room. Just remember that in organizing or de-cluttering your sewing room, the goal is to increase its functionality, boost your creativity and ensure your safety.

I have followed a step by step approach to help beginners to easily learn to sew. The basic devices and tools are also mentioned so that our readers can choose the most appropriate tool for the different types of fabrics and patterns they want to use. We hope our readers are now well versed in sewing terms and tools and are ready to begin their sewing adventures.

Good luck!

Made in the USA
Middletown, DE
27 January 2021